Becky May has led various children's and youth groups and programmes over the past 20 years, including Sunday morning discipleship groups for children aged 0–12 and midweek outreach groups for both primary-age children and teenagers. She was a primary school teacher for eight years, teaching in both Key Stage 1 and 2 and fulfilling leadership responsibilities, before leaving teaching to have her son, Isaac, in September 2012. More recently, the family has grown again following the arrival of baby Keziah. She has written for *Youthwork* magazine, YFC, Urban Saints, UCB and One Way UK, creating a variety of curriculum materials, articles, children's devotional materials and assembly scripts. Becky is also the Bedfordshire Regional Coordinator for Messy Church and cofounder of The Treasurebox People.

Published by
The Bible Reading Fellowship (BRF)
15 The Chambers, Vineyard
Abingdon OX14 3FE
United Kingdom
Tel: +44 (0)1865 319700
Email: enquiries@brf.org.uk
Website: www.brf.org.uk
BRF is a Registered Charity

ISBN 978 0 85746 381 4

First published 2016
10 9 8 7 6 5 4 3 2 1 0

Acknowledgements
Cover photo: © Thinkstock

Every effort has been made to trace and contact copyright owners for material used in this resource. We apologise for any inadvertent omissions or errors, and would ask those concerned to contact us so that full acknowledgement can be made in the future.

A catalogue record for this book is available from the British Library

Printed by Gutenberg Press, Tarxien, Malta

Important information

Photocopying permission

The right to photocopy material in *God's Story for Under 5s* is granted for the pages that contain the photocopying clause: 'Reproduced with permission from *God's Story for Under 5s* by Becky May (Barnabas for Children, 2016) www.barnabasinchurches.org.uk', so long as reproduction is for use in a teaching situation by the original purchaser. The right to photocopy material is not granted for anyone other than the original purchaser without written permission from BRF.

The Copyright Licensing Agency (CLA)

If you are resident in the UK and you have a photocopying licence with the Copyright Licensing Agency (CLA) please check the terms of your licence. If your photocopying request falls within the terms of your licence, you may proceed without seeking further permission. If your request exceeds the terms of your CLA licence, please contact the CLA directly with your request. Copyright Licensing Agency, Saffron House, 6–10 Kirby Street, London EC1N 8TS UK, Tel: 020 7400 3100, email cla@cla.co.uk; web www.cla.co.uk. The CLA will provide photocopying authorisation and royalty fee information on behalf of BRF.

The Bible Reading Fellowship (BRF) is a Registered Charity (233280).

Becky May

GOD'S STORY FOR UNDER 5s

36 Bible-based sessions for midweek and Sunday groups

Contents

Old Testament stories

New Testament stories

Introduction

This is the first in a series of three books, which can be used to provide a creative overview of some of the key stories in both the Old Testament and the New Testament, with primary and preschool-aged children. Each book can be used independently, if you are working with children in a particular age bracket, or you can combine this book with those for 5–7s and 7–11s, to enable all your children's groups to share these Bible stories in parallel with one another.

Who is this book for?

This curriculum has been prepared for anyone who wants to share God's big story with the smallest of children. It could be used as a year-long programme to work through the Bible week by week, throughout the academic year, or the appropriate stories may be used to celebrate key festivals in the church calendar, with other sessions slotted in as best suits your teaching plan for the year.

You can use it in a midweek play group, on a Sunday morning, or in nursery and preschool groups.

What does the book cover?

The 36 sessions, which run in sequence, work together to tell God's story from creation to Pentecost, telling many of the key stories of the faith along the way. Although there is not space to include every Bible story, it is hoped that the episodes selected will give your children and their families an overview of God's story and inspire you to adopt this style of learning and exploration as you continue with further Bible stories.

Activity areas

Each session includes a range of suggested activities, which are organised under the headings listed below. To enable children to experience the full depth and breadth of learning opportunities, it is hoped that you will be able to offer all of the suggested activities, immersing your group in the story of the day. Alternatively, if time and space are limited, you will need to select activities—but do try to take them from different areas each time, to ensure variety and to expose the children to different media and activity types. One of the key values of this curriculum is that children should have freedom of choice to select the activities that they want to participate in, and so, when space is limited, it is still important to offer variety and choice in the types of activities.

Included with the activities are suggestions of things to talk about with the children as they participate, if you have enough helpers available to lead or support children in their own discovery, play and learning. Parents and carers, if present, should also be invited to explore some of the activities with their children, as well as encouraging independent exploration.

Below you will find a short explanation of each activity area, with guidance on how to set up the environment for the best possible outcome.

Sensory, tactile, malleable

These activities offer children the chance to explore using their senses (often predominantly touch), as they handle and feel objects that relate to the story. Depending on the activity, you may need a table in this area, or a large tray, such as a builder's tray, known as a tuff spot.

Small world play

In this area, set up a model that relates to the story. Children can then manipulate figurines to act out the story, or play out a scenario that links the story to their own experiences. Because this activity usually involves small pieces, it will need to be set up in a quiet, protected area, such as at a table, off the floor.

Role play / dressing up

This area will give children the opportunity to act out for themselves something that relates to the story, retells the story, or explores an experience familiar to them, which will help them to understand the story better. This activity will work well in a larger area where children can have space to move around, perhaps with screens, with appropriate posters or pictures attached, to establish the environment better.

Creative

This is an area for arts and crafts where, through a range of media and techniques, children can make something simple to take home with them as a reminder of the session. This activity will work well at a table, where children can sit or stand around and easily access the materials that they need to use.

Construction

Using bricks and building blocks, wood and boxes, children can work (with help) to construct something, often on a large scale, that relates to the story. This activity is often used during the story time, as a prop for the retelling. You will need a large space for this activity, as it will often involve larger objects and can be quite noisy.

Books

Although most children in this age group are not yet readers, they will all exhibit a range of pre-reading skills and an interest in handling books for themselves. They might explore the illustrations and try to read independently, as well as having an adult who will read the books to them. Where possible, set up a reading rug or blanket, along with cushions, beanbags or chairs that children can sit on while they read the books. Display the books in such a way that children can access them independently.

Water

This activity will often work well with a water tray or water table, using appropriate tools or props relevant to the story. You will need to protect the surrounding area and supervise the activity to ensure that children explore the water area safely. Have cloths to hand to wipe up spillages.

Sand

This activity will require a sand tray or sand pit and a variety of sand tools to explore one aspect of the story. This is another activity area that may require more supervision.

Puzzles, toys, games

Under this heading, for each session, additional toys, games and puzzles are suggested, which can be offered to reinforce the learning that takes place in the session. These toys should be located where children can access them freely, perhaps on the floor or on a play mat, away from the more structured activities. It may be helpful to organise these activities by age or type.

Snack time

As you draw your free choice time to an end, gather the children and parents together for a small snack, offering drinks and cakes, biscuits or fruit. You could use this gathering time to celebrate birthdays and to share any notices or announcements you may have.

Story time

For each session, a script is provided so that you can tell the story in an interactive, creative way. Props or visual aids may be included, or the children may be involved in acting out parts of the story themselves.

Prayer

A short prayer is offered, which focuses on what we might learn from the story and gives children the opportunity to respond at an appropriate level. You may find it helpful to introduce the prayer by saying, 'I'm going to say a prayer. Please listen carefully and, if you want to join in, you can say "Amen" at the end.'

Songs

One or two songs and rhymes are suggested each time, relating to the theme of the session. You may wish to offer a selection of percussion instruments or ribbons and flags for the children to use, or teach them some simple actions to follow.

Take home

As you close your session, there is a suggested idea for an activity that families can participate in at home, to continue learning and growing together, or a simple object that children can take home as a physical reminder of the story and the things we can learn through it.

Old Testament stories

God creates the world

For the team

Refer to pages 6–8 to see how the activity areas work together

Session theme

This session explores the story of creation, enabling children to experience and enjoy access to many aspects of the beautiful world that God has created.

Bible text: Genesis 1—2

Team prayer

Thank you, God, for your beautiful creation, which you share with us all. Through this session, may the children experience for themselves your creativity, beauty and playfulness, as they play through the story with us today.

Activity areas

Sensory, tactile, malleable

Provide clay or play dough and invite the children and carers to mould and sculpt their own people. Encourage children to name each of the body parts as they make them, and to look at themselves and the other children, to copy the shapes that they see.

Talk about how we may all have the same body parts but we are all very different. Compare eye and hair colour, height and so on, as you work on your models and think about how God takes special care over everyone that he has made.

Small world play

Set up a tuff spot (builder's tray) as the garden of Eden, with small world play trees and plants and a selection of animal figures, along with a man and a woman figurine.

Talk about the beautiful world that God created and the way that Adam and Eve had to take care of all the animals he had made.

Creative

Present a selection of images of plants and flowers, or provide some small pot plants, as a stimulus for the children. Set up an easel and selection of paints to allow children to produce their own plant and flower paintings.

Talk about the huge variety of plants and flowers in the world, looking at the pictures you have provided. How many different colours and shapes can the children see?

Construction

Provide a large selection of cardboard boxes and other junk modelling materials that children and carers can use to design and create their own model animal. It could be a model of an animal that they already know about, such as a pet or favourite animal, or they may choose to invent their own creation.

Talk about the many different types of animal there are in the world. How many can the children name? Ask them to talk about their favourite animals and which animals they would most like to see.

Books

There is a huge scope for books that you could offer for this session. Ensure that you have books of the creation story available, along with age-appropriate children's Bibles. You could also offer books about people (such as people around the world or books that label body parts), books about animals and books about our world (which could include atlases and books about plants, oceans and even space).

Talk about the things that interest the children when they look at the books. Offer to read to any interested children, or simply talk about the pictures that they are looking at.

Water

Fill the water tray to an appropriate level and put a selection of toy fish and sea creatures into it. Encourage the children to play with them and to take them 'swimming through the sea'.

Talk about the fish and sea creatures that the children may have seen and those that live far out in the deepest oceans. God has made many, many beautiful creatures, all so very different from one another.

Sand

Provide some twigs with leaves on, which the children and carers can use to create 'trees' in the sand, as well as some small animal figures, along with a man and a woman figurine to look after the animals in the sand. Encourage the children to mould the sandy earth, to make places where the animals can live safely. Invite them to move the animals around, looking at the footprints they leave in the sand.

Talk about the way Adam and Eve could enjoy the garden that God had created and the responsibility they had for caring for all the animals.

Puzzles, toys, games

Give children access to any toys, puzzles and games that relate to the story. In particular, you may have a selection that are animal themed or space themed, or that relate to human beings and body parts.

Snack time

Story time

The story for this session is told through the use of visual aids, built up layer by layer to show how God created the world. A number of props are needed. If you have a small group, you could sit everybody in a circle and display the props on the floor in the centre (as directed in the script below). For larger groups, you may wish to display the props as a banner that is hung in front of them. If you are using the up-front banner style of storytelling, you will need to prepare the props to enable them to be attached to one another.

Sit everyone down and start telling the story.

This morning we have been thinking about the beautiful world that God created. This is the story of how God created our world, which is told to us at the very beginning of the Bible.

A long, long time ago, before there were people and animals, birds and trees, there was nothing but God.

Place a large circle of black fabric on the floor in the middle of the circle.

God spoke. He said, 'Light', and suddenly light appeared.

Place a smaller circle of shiny white, silver or yellow fabric just outside the black circle.

God spoke again. He said, 'Sky' and 'Sea', and out of nothing God made the skies and the seas.

Cover the top half of the black circle with a light blue fabric and the bottom half with a darker blue fabric.

Then God said, 'Earth', and the seas were split by the land that God had created.

Cover one quadrant of the dark blue 'sea' with a green piece of fabric.

'Growing things,' said God, and there appeared plants, trees and beautiful flowers.

Sprinkle pictures or felt cut-out shapes over the green fabric.

God spoke again: 'Day and night.'

In one half of the light blue 'sky', place a sun image, and, in the other half, a moon and stars.

'Living things,' said God. 'Animals and birds, fish and human beings.'

As you name them, place images into the appropriate sections of the circle, encouraging the children to name the creatures that you include.

God had finished making his beautiful world. 'Perfect,' he said as he looked at everything he had made. When he had finished, he took a rest and enjoyed his beautiful world.

Prayer

Thank you, God, for the beautiful world that you created. Thank you for the sun, moon and stars, the land and the sea, the animals, fish and birds, and thank you for creating me. Amen

Songs

Songs today could include:

- Father God created the world (Ian Smale)
- He's got the whole world in his hands (Anon)

Take home

Suggest that your families take a walk outdoors and enjoy God's creation together.

2

Adam and Eve make a bad choice

For the team

Refer to pages 6–8 to see how the activity areas work together

Session theme

This session explores what happened when Adam and Eve chose to eat the fruit that the snake offered them. Within this session, we will consider the choices that we all make on a daily basis—whether to do what we know is right or not.

Bible text: Genesis 3

Team prayer

Father God, today, as we explore the story of Adam and Eve, help us to share the need to make good choices with the children and families, as well as your message of forgiveness.

Activity areas

Sensory, tactile, malleable

Cook some spaghetti or linguini before the session, possibly dyed in food colouring, and place it in a large container, adding a small amount of oil to prevent the pasta from sticking together. Encourage the children and carers to weave the pasta between their fingers, twist it around their wrists and wiggle it along the surface of the table.

Talk about the way that snakes slither on their bellies. Can the children slither their spaghetti snakes along in a wriggly line?

Small world play

Set up the garden of Eden in the tuff spot, as in the previous session, with small world play trees and plants and a selection of animal figures, along with a man and a woman figurine. Today, introduce a snake to the scene and place a tree (perhaps a slightly larger one) right in the middle of the garden.

Talk about the snake in the garden. Explain that snakes are not intrinsically bad creatures, even though some snakes are dangerous, but that the snake in today's story represents evil or badness.

Role play / dressing up

Create a garden scene with wheelbarrows, hand tools, aprons, flower pots, real or artificial flowers held in oasis floral foam, watering cans and gardening gloves. Encourage the children and carers to act out the role of gardeners, taking care of the plants in the garden.

Talk about the way that God gave Adam and Eve the job of caring for his beautiful creation. God wanted them to be able to enjoy his beautiful world, but they did not do the right thing.

Creative

Provide a variety of different fruits, cut in half, to be used for printing. Apples, pears, satsuma segments, grapes and strawberries all work well. (Remember to check for food allergies, and ensure that the children do not put painted pieces of fruit in their mouths.) Set out poster paints in a range of colours, large sheets of paper and painting aprons. Invite the children and carers to create prints of the different fruits, drawing attention to the different shapes that they form.

Talk about the different fruits—their names, tastes and textures. Do the children have a favourite fruit?

Construction

Work together with the children to construct a large tree. This can be done in a number of different ways, such as using a long, thick cardboard tube as the trunk and creating branches from rolled-up newspaper or long sticks, or creating a trunk in advance of the session from chicken wire, which can be covered in papier mâché during the session. If possible, go outside to collect leaves or make them from green paper to attach to the branches of the tree.

Talk about the different types of tree that children have seen. Tell them that in the story today they will hear about a very special tree.

Books

Offer a range of non-fiction books about snakes and trees, along with the children's Bibles and creation story books that you had available for the previous session, to encourage children to see the continuity of the story.

Some children may like to have the books read to them, or may enjoy sharing the pictures with an adult.

Sand

Set up the sand tray with an area of wet sand and an area of dry sand. Provide a number of rubber snakes that children can drag through both the wet and dry sand to see the tracks that the snakes leave behind.

Talk about the way that snakes slither on their bellies, rather than walking on feet like we and most other animals do. Talk about the prints that the snakes leave behind them.

Puzzles, toys, games

Among the toys and games offered today, you could include an age-appropriate version of the game Snakes and Ladders, perhaps using a large floor-mat version.

Snack time

Story time

For the story today, use the small world scene created in the tuff spot. Invite children and their carers to sit in a circle around the scene so that they can all see the story as it is played out before them. Use a male and a female figurine to represent Adam and Eve, but take the snake out of the scene for the beginning of the story. Point to or move the figures as appropriate in the course of the story.

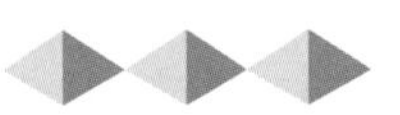

Look at this beautiful world that God created. Last week we heard all about the way that God made his beautiful creation. Today, we're going to find out what happened next.

God was very pleased with his creation. He loved Adam and Eve and wanted to share his beautiful world with them. God told Adam and Eve that he wanted them to help to look after the plants and the animals. He said that they could play in the garden and that they could enjoy eating the fruit that grew on the trees—all except for the fruit on this one tree.

It was a bit like when Mummy says we mustn't touch the oven or the iron. God wanted to keep Adam and Eve safe, just as your parents want to keep you safe. The trouble was, Adam and Eve didn't follow God's rule, just as sometimes we don't do what our mummies and daddies say.

One day, when Eve was in the garden, close to the tree that she knew God had told her not to touch, she saw a snake. But this was no ordinary snake; this snake spoke! He said to Eve, 'What did God say about eating the fruit that grows on the trees?'

Eve told the snake that they were allowed to eat from any of the trees except for this one. Then the snake tricked Eve. 'That's not fair!' he said. 'God doesn't want you to be as clever as he is—that's why he doesn't want you to eat this fruit. Go on... eat the fruit. It will be good.'

Eve had a choice to make. She could have chosen to do the right thing and leave the fruit alone, but Eve chose to do what the snake told her instead, and she ate the fruit. She thought it was delicious and she told Adam to eat the fruit too.

The trouble was, the snake had tricked Adam and Eve, and Adam and Eve had both done the wrong thing by breaking God's rule. God was very sad because Adam and Eve had made a bad choice. God still loved Adam and Eve, but from now on they would have to work hard and they couldn't enjoy playing in God's beautiful world as they had done before.

Prayer

Dear God, sometimes we make bad choices, like Adam and Eve did, and we're sorry for the times when we get things wrong. Thank you that you always love us. Please help us to make good choices. Amen

Songs

Songs today could include:

- I can do all things (Jim Bailey)
- If I've been wrong (Sammy Horner)

Take home

You could suggest that your families create a behaviour chart, perhaps with a fruit tree as a picture, to focus on making good choices in the week ahead.

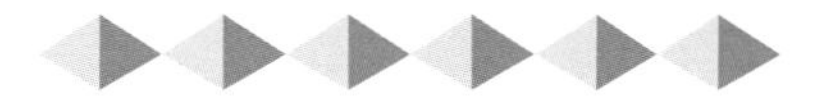

3

Noah and the ark

For the team

Refer to pages 6–8 to see how the activity areas work together

Session theme

During this session, children will explore the story of Noah's ark and God's plan to give the world a fresh start. As well as activities about animals and boat building, the teaching today focuses on God's promise never to flood the world again.

Bible text: Genesis 6—9

Team prayer

Dear God, in the midst of animals and raindrops, boat building and the rainbow, help us to share the story of your love and your second chance for this planet that you love.

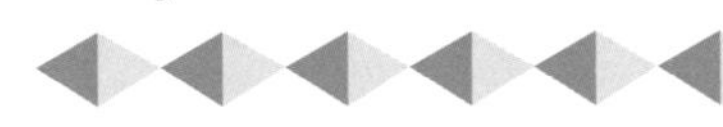

Activity areas

Sensory, tactile, malleable

Prepare some play dough in a range of colours and invite children and carers to create a small model of their favourite animal, ready to use during the story time. Keep a list of the animals that children choose to make, to avoid having more than two of each animal.

Talk about how different all the animals are that God created, with their different shapes and colours. How amazing it must have been for Noah when all the animals came on board the ark!

Small world play

A number of 'Noah's ark' toys are available to purchase, which would work well for this activity. Alternatively, provide a number of small animal figures in pairs, along with a cardboard box, out of which you can form a basic ark shape.

Talk about the names of the different animals, the noises they make and the physical features that the children notice. What do the children think it would have been like on the ark, surrounded by all those noisy animals?

Role play / dressing up

Create an area where the children can take care of some animals, as they would at a vet's or animal rehoming centre, for example. You could include a selection of stuffed toy animals, brushes for grooming, food and water bowls, baskets or cardboard boxes with blankets, where the animals can sleep. Children may also like to dress up as vets or wear aprons for this activity.

Talk about the things you need to do to take care of an animal. Children may have experience of taking care of a pet, so encourage them to talk about those experiences. How would Noah and his family have cared for all the animals on the ark?

Creative

Before the session, cut paper plates into two halves and provide colouring pens or paints in each of the colours of the rainbow. Show children how to colour or paint their own rainbow, using the curve of the plate to shape the curved bands. They need to start with red on the outside edge of the plate and work towards the centre, concluding with a violet band.

Talk about how rainbows appear in the sky sometimes after it has been raining. God painted the first rainbow in the sky after the flood as a sign of his promise that he would never flood the earth again.

Construction

Many preschool settings incorporate woodworking activities into their programmes. There will need to be a thorough risk assessment to cover this activity, but, once appropriate safety measures have been taken, children and carers can help to 'build the ark' in this area. They can sandpaper wood to make it smooth, hammer nails into wood, put screws into the wood (adults should start them off for the children), and even saw wood held in a vice. Softwoods work best for this activity and activities will need to be completed under close supervision.

Talk about the things you can make with wood and what you have to do to the wood as you work with it. How hard did Noah have to work to build his ark?

Books

Include a selection of children's Bibles and story books about Noah and the ark, along with non-fiction books about animals, boats and weather.

Read the books to any children who choose to listen, or discuss the pictures that they find interesting.

Water

Fill the water tray to a halfway point and provide some plastic boats for children to float on the water. Plastic animals could also be provided to put into the boats, along with watering cans to pour 'rain' over the floating boats.

Talk about what it would have been like for Noah and his family to be on board the ark for such a long time, without being able to step on to dry land. How would they have felt? What would they have missed the most about life on dry land?

Puzzles, toys, games

A number of Noah's ark themed toys can be sourced for use in this session, such as jigsaw puzzles, stacking cubes and shape sorters. In addition, games that involve finding 'pairs' or matching cards or objects with a partner could be offered, along with other generic animal-themed toys and games.

Snack time

Story time

For this story retelling, you will need a model or toy Noah's ark (created from a cardboard box, if no other model is available), along with people figurines to represent Noah and his family. Invite the children to sit around in a circle with the play dough animals they have made, ready to use in the story.

Some time after God had created his beautiful world, he looked around at all the people and was very sad. There were lots of people who were unkind, who did wrong things and upset other people. Then God noticed Noah *(point to the figure)*. Noah and his family were good people who tried to make God happy by doing the right thing. God had a plan to keep Noah and his family safe but to get rid of all the people who did wrong, so that the world could have a fresh start.

God told Noah to build an ark—a very, very big boat. Then Noah had to bring two of every kind of animal on to the boat. There were giraffes and lions, sheep and cats...

Refer to the list of animals that the children have created and invite them to bring each animal, as you mention it, to put on to the ark.

When all the animals were safely on board, the doors were shut. Then the rain started.

Encourage the children and carers to gently tap their fingertips on the ground to represent the rain.

It rained for one day, two days, three days, four days... It rained for 40 whole days and nights, and the ark sailed, with all the noisy animals on board, until suddenly it stopped raining.

Gently, gently, the water started to go down. When all the water had gone, God told Noah to take his family and the animals out of the ark and on to dry land. Then God painted a beautiful rainbow in the sky. The rainbow was God's promise that he would never send such a big flood again, and he never ever has.

Prayer

Dear God, we're sorry for the times when we are unkind and hurt other people. Thank you that you always give us another chance to do the right thing. Thank you for beautiful rainbows, which remind us that you keep your promises. Amen

Songs

Songs and rhymes today could include 'Mr Noah built an ark' (to the tune of 'Old MacDonald'):

Mr Noah built an ark, e-i-e-i-o.
And on the ark he took two...

Invite children to suggest which animals they want to sing about, perhaps asking them to choose animals for which they already know the animal noise.

Take home

Encourage your families to play a game of Pairs or Snap with animal playing cards at home. Suggest that they keep their eyes out for rainbows as a reminder of God's promise.

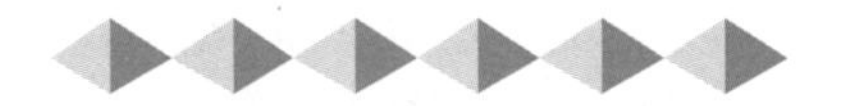

God's promise to Abraham and Sarah

For the team

Refer to pages 6–8 to see how the activity areas work together

Session theme

The story of Abraham weaves through many twists and turns, but this session focuses on God's promise to Abraham and Sarah that they would have many descendants, and on the subsequent birth of Isaac.

Bible text: Genesis 15; 17:1—18:15; 21:1–7

Team prayer

Thank you, God, that you always keep your promises, even when we have to wait many years to see them come to fruition. Help us to share this truth with the families that we meet today.

Activity areas

Sensory, tactile, malleable

Fill a tuff spot or tray with a thick layer of black beans and place a number of glow-in-the-dark stars into the tray. Encourage children to use their hands to feel through the beans and find the stars, counting them as they do so.

Talk about the sky at night and the way that stars shine brightly in the dark. God told Abraham that one day there would be more people in his family than there are stars in the sky, more than we could possibly count.

Small world play

Provide a selection of small wooden posts, sticks or plastic drinking straws and small pieces of fabric that can be used to create a tent scene. Use more sticks to build a camp fire, and provide people and appropriate animal figures to inhabit the scene.

Talk about the way that people lived in the time of Abraham and Sarah, sleeping in tents with their animals close by.

Role play / dressing up

Create a home scene, where children can take care of a baby. You could provide dolls, dolls' clothes, nappies, toy bottles, blankets, a cot and a toy pram, for example.

Talk about children's experiences of helping to look after a baby, perhaps a sibling or cousin. What do they enjoy most about helping with a baby? Is there anything they do not like doing?

Creative

Provide some star shapes cut from card and a selection of glitters, glitter glues and sequins, along with a hole punch and thread with which to hang the stars. Invite children to decorate their own sparkly stars to hang up as a reminder of today's story.

Talk about the way that stars shine in the night sky. Ask the children if they have ever tried to count all the stars that they can see at night.

Construction

Use a variety of frames, such as laundry dryers, poles, tables and chairs, as well as blankets and sheets, to build some tents together. Ensure that all structures are stable before children get under them, but try to involve children in the construction process.

Talk about children's experiences of spending the night in a tent. Can they imagine what it would be like to live in a tent all the time?

Books

Offer a selection of children's Bibles and books about Abraham, Sarah and Isaac, as well as other books about babies, camping and tents, and the night sky.

Offer to read these books to the children. Share anything that they find interesting in the books as they look at them.

Water

Provide a baby bath filled with water to an appropriate level, a plastic doll, towels and a small quantity of toiletries for a baby (remembering to check for allergies). Help the children to give the baby doll a bath.

Talk about the way that you bathe a baby safely. Has anyone helped to do this before? Perhaps one or two leaders or parents could help by talking about bathing their young babies.

Sand

Provide dry sand in the sand tray for this session, along with sieves, pouring cups and sand wheels for children to pour the sand through.

Talk about the amount of sand in the sand tray. Is it possible to count the grains of sand as they fall through the equipment back into the tray? God told Abraham that one day there would be more people in his family than there are grains of sand on the beach.

Puzzles, toys, games

Source some pictures of different constellations in the sky or create your own, using star stickers stuck on to black card. Encourage the children to count the stars in each of the pictures, perhaps by putting a counter on to each star.

Snack time

Story time

Prepare two pictures to use as prompts for the children—a smiley face and a sad face. Explain that when they see the sad face, they should pretend to cry, and when the smiley face is shown, they should pretend to laugh. You will also need a doll wrapped in a blanket, to be brought out at the

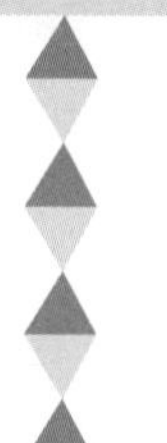

appropriate moment in the story. Ask a volunteer to play the part of Sarah and to sit on a stool at the edge of the tent that you created earlier in the session. Invite the children to come and sit around or even inside the tent, and begin the story.

A long, long time ago, there was a lady called Sarah *(point to your volunteer)* and a man called Abraham. They lived in a tent, a bit like this one, surrounded by their animals and servants. Sarah and Abraham were good friends with God. God had made a promise to Abraham, many years before, that one day they would have a family of their own. God had said there would be more people in their family than there are stars in the sky or grains of sand on the beach.

Sarah and Abraham waited a very long time, but God did not seem to give them what he had promised—there was no baby. This made Sarah very sad *(show the sad face)*.

One day, some visitors came to Sarah and Abraham's tent. They told Abraham that Sarah would have a baby, just as God had promised. Sarah heard this and she thought it was very silly, because she was so old. It made her laugh and laugh *(show the smiley face)*.

But even though Sarah and Abraham were very old, God kept his promise. One year later, Sarah did have a baby, just as God had promised she would. Sarah and Abraham named their baby Isaac, which means 'laughter' *(show the smiley face)*, because God had made them very happy.

Prayer

Thank you, God, for our families, who keep us safe and look after us, just like Abraham and Sarah looked after Isaac. Thank you that you always keep your promises, even when we have to wait a long time. Amen

Songs

Songs today could include:

- Father Abraham had many sons (Anon)

Take home

Give each family a glow-in-the-dark star to take home with them, to put on display where their whole family will notice it. The star will remind them that God always keeps his promises, just as he did for Abraham and Sarah.

Joseph is taken to Egypt

For the team

Refer to pages 6–8 to see how the activity areas work together

Session theme

This is the first of two sessions that explore the life of Joseph, beginning this week with Joseph's relationship with his brothers and how he found his way to Egypt.

Bible text: Genesis 37

Team prayer

Dear God, as we explore family relationships in today's session, help us to nurture positive relationships between parents, children and siblings. Help us to share the truth that you want the best for each member of our families and are watching over us all.

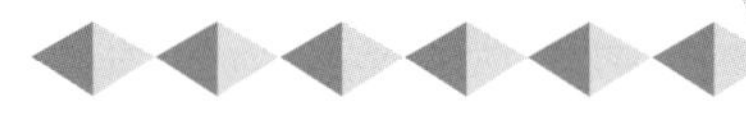

Activity areas

Sensory, tactile, malleable

Gather together a selection of brightly coloured ribbons and a large piece of mesh or netting with holes wide enough for children to weave the ribbons in and out.

Talk about the way that Joseph's father had a special, brightly coloured coat made for his son, to show how much he loved Joseph.

Small world play

Provide a selection of dressing-up dolls and various clothing items, and encourage the children to choose clothes for the dolls to wear. You could also provide some fabric scraps in a range of colours and patterns, so that the children can make their own clothes for the dolls.

Talk about the different clothes that the children choose for the dolls. What clothes do they like to choose to wear? Can they get dressed by themselves or do they need help? Would they like someone to make an outfit for them to wear?

Role play / dressing up

Gather a range of 'special' clothes for children to try on. They could include party or bridesmaid dresses, hats, waistcoats, saris and a selection of jewellery items.

Talk about times when the children have worn special clothes, such as for a party or wedding. Ask the children if they have ever had special clothes made for them, as Joseph did.

Creative

In advance of the session, cut out some simple coat shapes from white card. Provide some paper squares in a range of colours, patterns and textures; such as sugar paper, tissue paper, foil and so on. Encourage the children and carers to stick the paper squares all over the coat shape, using PVA glue, to create their own Joseph coat.

Talk about all the different colours, patterns and textures that the children notice and choose. Can they find any of the same colours or patterns in their own clothes?

Books

Among the books offered today, include stories and information books about families, along with books about colours and stars. Offer a selection of children's Bibles and story books about Joseph.

Share the books with the children, offering to read to any children who wish to hear the stories or talk about the non-fiction books.

Water

Set up a well by surrounding the water tray or a paddling pool with a large cardboard box or pieces of card. Tie a bucket on to a length of rope, so that children and carers can use it to fetch the water.

Talk about the way that Joseph and his brothers would have had to collect all their water from a well like this. Joseph's brothers found a dry well, where there was no water left, where they could leave Joseph.

Sand

Provide spades and invite the children and carers to dig deep holes in the sand.

Talk about the way that Joseph's brothers first hid him in a deep hole in the field while they decided what to do with him. How must Joseph have felt when his brothers threw him into the hole?

Puzzles, toys, games

Among the toys offered today, include colour-matching games and different coloured beads for threading and creating patterns. This session can also make use of the star counting cards that were created for the Abraham and Sarah themed session.

Snack time

Story time

You will need twelve people shapes for the story today. They could be cut from paper, card or wood, but should be very plain and simple. You will need a simple card coat shape, coloured brightly, which can be attached to and removed from one of the characters at the appropriate points in the story, as well as eleven small stars, a moon and a sun. Invite the families to sit in a circle around the area where you will tell the story.

There was once a man called Jacob, who had twelve sons *(point to each of the figures, counting them as you do so)*. He loved all of his sons, but he did love one more than all the others. Joseph was Jacob's favourite son. Joseph's brothers thought this wasn't fair and they were very jealous of their brother.

Once, to show how much he loved Joseph, Jacob made him a very special coat to wear *(attach the coat to the eleventh character to represent Joseph)*. Look! It was very beautiful—red and blue, green and yellow. Joseph's brothers weren't very happy about it. They were jealous that Joseph had been given such a special present, and they had nothing!

Another time, Joseph told his brothers about the dreams he had. In one dream, he dreamt that the sun, the moon and eleven stars all bowed down to him *(place Joseph at the centre of the scene and place each of the stars above the heads of the other figures)*. Now Joseph's brothers were really angry! Why did he think he was so important?

One day, while his brothers were out in the field *(move the stars, moon and sun away, and set the figures to one side of the scene, with Joseph at the other side)*, Joseph's father sent him out to check on his brothers *(move Joseph towards the other people)*.

Joseph's brothers saw their chance to get rid of him. They tore his special coat off him *(remove the coat)*, found a well and threw him into it. They saw some men travelling past on their way to Egypt and they sold Joseph to them as a slave *(remove Joseph from the scene)*.

Then the brothers took Joseph's coat home to their dad, Jacob. They lied to him and told him that Joseph had been killed by a wild animal. Jacob was very sad. He missed Joseph very much, but God was looking after Joseph and had a special plan for his life.

Prayer

Thank you, God, for our families—our brothers and sisters, our mums and dads. We're sorry for the times when we argue, like Joseph and his brothers did. Help us to show our family that we love them all very much. Amen

Songs

Songs today could include:

- Big family of God (Becky Drake)
- Our God is a great big God (Nigel and Jo Hemming)

Take home

Suggest that your families spend some time this week talking about why each member of their family is special.

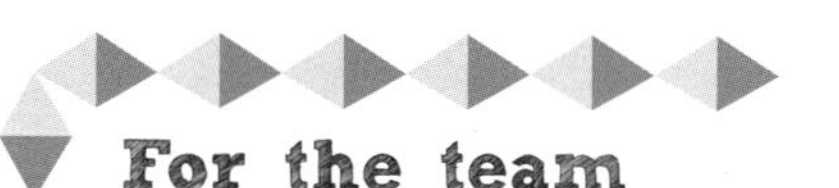

6 Joseph serves God

For the team

Refer to pages 6–8 to see how the activity areas work together

Session theme

This is the second of two sessions that explore the life of Joseph, picking up at the point where he finds himself in Egypt. It focuses on his God-given ability to interpret dreams, and how God used this to raise him up in Egypt to a place of honour.

Bible text: Genesis 39—45

Team prayer

Dear God, thank you for the drama and action of today's story. Help us to relate Joseph's 'larger-than-life' story to the children's own experiences as we share the truth that you are always with us, in every circumstance.

Activity areas

Sensory, tactile, malleable

Provide a number of grapes for children to taste and to squish and squeeze between their fingers. Are they able to squeeze any juice out of the grapes?

Talk about the way that wine is made by squeezing the juice out of grapes. When Joseph was in prison, he met Pharaoh's wine taster, who would have prepared the wine for Pharaoh.

Small world play

Create a farm scene with a number of different shaped and sized model cows. Encourage the children to come and sort the cows by size, from the smallest to the largest.

Talk about Pharaoh, who had a dream about cows. God told Joseph what the dream meant and he was able to help Pharaoh to make sure that his people had enough food to eat.

Role play / dressing up

Divide your role play area into two spaces to show the different places where Joseph found himself. Set up a 'prison cell', perhaps using a play pen or a large box with a doorway cut into it, or just a blanket or two. Then set up a 'royal palace' with a throne and crowns, or Egyptian headdresses, jewellery, mirrors and other expensive-looking luxuries.

Talk about the way that God made it possible for Joseph to be let out of prison, to be given a special job in Pharaoh's palace. God was always looking after Joseph, no matter where he was.

Creative

Provide a selection of seeds and grains, sheets of card and PVA glue, which the children can use to create their own seed pictures. You could also provide pencils and stencils to create an outline shape to fill with the grains.

Talk about how Joseph told Pharaoh to save the extra grain that grew, so that the Egyptians would have enough food to eat when the famine came.

Construction

Provide a selection of building bricks and invite the children and carers to build storehouses to keep the grain secure. You could provide a bag of grain or seed for the children to pour into their storehouses to check how effective they are.

Talk about how Joseph advised Pharaoh to build big barns, or storehouses, where they could keep some of the harvest, to make sure that they would have enough food when the bad harvests came.

Books

Offer a variety of children's Bibles and story books about Joseph, alongside age-appropriate non-fiction books about Egypt for children to look at and share together.

Talk about the things the children notice from the illustrations in the books and offer to read the books to the children as they wish.

Water

Provide a selection of different cups, beakers, bottles and jugs and encourage children and carers to pour water from a jug into a cup. Consider including plastic wine goblets as one type of cup for the children to use.

Talk about how Joseph met Pharaoh's wine taster while he was in prison. It was the wine taster's job to serve wine to the king. Can the children pour the water as though they were serving the king?

Puzzles, toys, games

You could offer children some farm-related toys to play with today, such as tractors and trailers, as well as toys or puzzles with an Egyptian theme.

Snack time

Story time

For today's story, make use of the scenery created for the role play area, with a 'prison' area and a 'palace' area. Invite the children and carers to sit in front of the scenery, and invite volunteers to play the following roles: Joseph, the jailer, the wine taster and Pharaoh.

Do you remember how we heard the story of Joseph and his brothers last week? Joseph was sold as a slave to people who were going to Egypt, where he got a job working for an Egyptian family. Things were going well for Joseph until he was tricked and put into prison.

Ask the jailer to lead Joseph to the 'prison' area.

While Joseph was in prison, God helped him to understand what people's dreams meant. One day, a new prisoner was brought to the prison. This man worked for the king of Egypt, the Pharaoh. He was a wine taster, someone who served wine to Pharaoh.

Ask the jailer to lead the wine taster to the 'prison' area.

While he was in prison, the wine taster had a very strange dream about his job. He dreamt that he was squeezing the grapes to make wine for Pharaoh again. Joseph helped him to understand the dream. Joseph told the man that it meant he would get out of prison and would get his old job back again.

The man's dream came true. He was released from prison and went back to work for Pharaoh again.

The wine taster should move to the 'palace' area, where Pharaoh is sitting.

When he was working again, the wine taster heard that Pharaoh had been having some strange dreams. He told Pharaoh that he knew someone in prison who could help him to understand his dreams—Joseph. Pharaoh told the jailer to fetch Joseph to him.

Joseph should now move to the 'palace' area.

Pharaoh told Joseph all about his strange dream, which was about skinny cows eating fat cows. Joseph asked God what it meant. Then Joseph told Pharaoh—his dream was a warning that Egypt was going to have a famine, which meant there would be no food. Pharaoh invited Joseph to help him to look after his people, storing up food for them to eat when the famine started and the crops would not grow.

Joseph listened to God and did what he said. Because of this, he was freed from prison, given a very important job and saved the Egyptians from starving. God even brought Joseph's family to Egypt so that they could forgive each other and be together again.

Prayer

Dear God, thank you that you have a plan for each of our lives, just as you did for Joseph. Please help us to listen to you and to hear what you want us to do. Amen

Songs

Songs today could include:

- Our God is a great big God (Nigel and Jo Hemming)

Take home

Encourage your families to talk about the way that God is looking after them, whatever situation they find themselves in at present.

The baby in the basket

For the team

Refer to pages 6–8 to see how the activity areas work together

Session theme

This is the first of three sessions that explore the life of Moses, beginning this week with the story of his birth and rescue by the princess. It will remind the children that God will always look after us.

Bible text: Exodus 2:1–10

Team prayer

Dear God, as we explore the life of Moses over the next few weeks, help us to share the message that you are with us always and will take care of us in every situation.

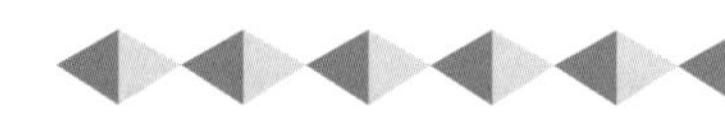

Activity areas

Sensory, tactile, malleable

Gather some long strips of fabric in a range of colours and textures. They could include fur, fleece, cotton, satin and hessian, along with some wide ribbons. Set out a plastic washing basket with holes in it, and invite children to come and weave the strips of fabric in and out of the holes in the basket.

Talk about the way that Moses' mother made a basket to put him in, by weaving reeds together.

Small world play

Set up a dolls' house, including a nursery with a baby, cot, pram and other appropriate baby-related items. Encourage the children to play out family life with a new baby, alongside other family members if present.

Talk about how family members all help to look after a new baby. Encourage the children to share their own experiences of having a new baby in the family and the ways they might help to look after them. Moses' mother and sister worked together to look after baby Moses.

Role play / dressing up

Create a nursery scene, with baby dolls in prams, pushchairs, cots or perhaps Moses baskets. Provide small nappies and wet wipes, baby clothes, blankets and disused baby bottles. Encourage the children to take care of the babies, changing, feeding and cuddling them as necessary.

Talk about the different things that babies need and the way that we take care of them.

Creative

Provide cornflakes, chocolate, cake cases, ready-rolled icing and jelly babies. Safely melt the chocolate before allowing the children to help mix in the cornflakes. Spoon a small quantity into each cake case, using the spoon to create a small hollow in the middle of the mixture. Take a small piece of icing, roll it flat and wrap it around a jelly baby to create a blanket, before placing the baby into the chocolate basket.

Talk about the way that Moses' mother carefully wrapped him in a blanket before putting him into the basket. How do the children think she would have felt as she put him in the basket?

Construction

Gather a large collection of boxes and invite the children to work together to build a square-based pyramid. Encourage the children to count the blocks as they use them and help them to make each layer smaller than the previous layer.

Talk about how the Egyptian pharaohs used slaves to build the pyramids and other buildings.

Books

Display a selection of age-appropriate non-fiction books about Egypt, rivers and babies, along with children's Bibles and story books about Moses.

Share the stories and books with the children as they wish, and talk about the things that they notice and find interesting in the stories and illustrations.

Water

Provide a range of different containers made from a variety of different materials, such as plastic trays, cardboard boxes, cooking tins and woven baskets. Allow the children and carers to explore which containers float and which ones sink.

Talk about the way that Moses' mother would have prepared the basket to make sure her baby boy would be safe and would not sink into the river.

Puzzles, toys, games

Toys and games included today could have a baby-related theme—perhaps additional small world play toys with family figurines. You could also provide games and puzzles with a river theme, perhaps including fish and boats.

Snack time

Story time

Kneel on the floor in front of the children for this story retelling, and have the following props positioned next to you, to use as you tell the story: a baby doll, a blanket, a basket and a large piece of blue fabric.

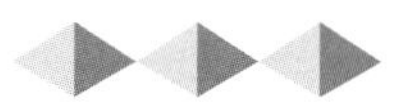

Do you remember how we heard about Joseph and his family and how they all found their way to live in Egypt? A long time after Joseph and his family lived in Egypt, there were lots of their great-grandchildren living there. They were called the Israelites and they were God's own people.

One day, a new Egyptian pharaoh, or king, came into power. He didn't like the Israelites. He made them work very hard, but he was scared that soon there would be so many Israelites that they would take over Egypt. He made a new rule—a very sad rule. He wanted all the Israelite baby boys to be killed as soon as they were born, so that they could not take over his country.

There was an Israelite woman who had a beautiful baby boy.

Take the doll in your arms.

She loved him very much and wanted to keep him safe. God wanted to keep this baby safe too. The woman made a plan to protect her baby and asked God to keep him safe.

So she wrapped him in a blanket and carefully put him into a basket.

Wrap the doll and place it in the basket. Then put the basket to one side as you spread the blue cloth out in front of you.

She took the basket down to the river and carefully put it into the water, where it could float. Then she told the baby's big sister to hide close by, to watch what happened.

The big sister watched her baby brother, and so did God. God was keeping this baby safe. As the sister watched, Pharaoh's daughter, a princess, came down to the river to wash. While she was in the water, the princess noticed the basket and went to look inside. She was amazed when she opened the basket to find a baby inside.

Lift the doll out of the basket to cuddle it.

The princess decided that she wanted to keep this baby safe too. She spotted the baby's big sister near the river and sent her to find someone to look after the baby, who she called Moses. His sister went to find his mum, who was given the special job of looking after baby Moses until he was old enough to live at the palace.

Moses was looked after and kept safe, all thanks to his mum, his sister, a princess and God, who was watching over them all.

Prayer

Thank you, God, that you looked after Moses and kept him safe. Thank you that you look after us too and we can trust you to keep us safe. Amen

Songs

Songs today could include the following adaptation of 'Rock-a-bye baby':

Rock-a-bye baby
There on the Nile.
When the wind blows
The basket shall rock.
When the princess
Comes down to the Nile,
She'll take him in
And keep the babe safe.

Take home

Encourage the families to spend some time looking at their family baby photos and talk about their memories of having babies in the families.

Escape from Egypt

For the team

Refer to pages 6–8 to see how the activity areas work together

Session theme

This is the second of three sessions that explore the life of Moses, today picking up at the time of the exodus. Through this session, we focus on the concept of God bringing freedom to his people, and remind the children of God's ongoing care for us in every circumstance.

Bible text: Exodus 5—14

Team prayer

Dear God, as we continue to explore the life of Moses, help us to enjoy your great gift of freedom and to share again the message that you care for all your people.

Activity areas

Sensory, tactile, malleable

Provide air-drying clay and a selection of small tools including rolling pins and cutters. Invite the children to use the tools to create small brick shapes out of the clay, which they can then use to build into walls.

Talk about how the Israelite slaves had to work very long days in the hot sun for the Egyptians, making bricks to use for building houses.

Small world play

Use a selection of small mini-beast figurines to create a mini-beast garden, including frogs, flies, gnats and locusts or other available insects. Gather a variety of leaves, small sticks and moss to create a suitable habitat to play with the mini-beasts in their 'home'.

Talk about how God sent huge swarms of these creatures to Egypt to try to persuade Pharaoh to let the Israelites leave Egypt—but Pharaoh would not listen. Explain that we do not need to be afraid of these creatures. God sent thousands and thousands of them, not one or two, like we might see.

Role play / dressing up

Create a dark den, using a very large cardboard box or a tent or pop-up shelter, with a thick, dark-coloured blanket thrown over the top to make it darker inside. You can introduce a light source with a line of fairy lights or battery-operated lights or torches.

Talk about how God made Egypt dark to try to persuade Pharaoh to listen to Moses and let the Israelites escape from Egypt—but Pharaoh wouldn't listen. Talk about how the children feel about the dark and reassure them that we don't need to be afraid of the dark.

Creative

Provide small paper plates so that children and carers can create a paper plate frog. Begin by painting the plate green, then draw around the children's hands on to green card, cut out the shapes and glue them near to the bottom of the plate. When the paint is dry, use a black felt-tip pen to draw eyes and a mouth near the top of the plate.

Talk about how God had to send many warnings to Pharaoh before he would listen, and one of these warnings was a swarm of jumping frogs.

Books

Offer children a selection of children's Bibles and story books about Moses, along with the books about Egypt that were available in the previous session.

Share the books with the children, reading to any children who want you to, and sharing the illustrations together.

Water

Provide a selection of cups, jugs and spoons in the water tray. Invite the children and carers to try to divide the water into two parts. Encourage them to try any of the tools that they think may be able to separate the water.

Talk about how we cannot divide water, as liquid will always fill the space it is given. In today's story, though, we hear how God separated the water into two parts, so that the Israelites could walk straight through. Only God could perform this miracle.

Sand

Collect rectangular containers, such as margarine tubs, which children can use as moulds to create brick shapes from wet sand.

Talk about how the Israelites had to make bricks from clay mixed with straw. When our sand bricks dry out, they will crumble, but the clay bricks went hard, ready for building houses.

Puzzles, toys, games

Among the toys offered today, provide some jumping frogs. Show the children how they can make them jump by applying pressure to the back of the frog's body and then releasing it.

Snack time

Story time

The story for this session involves a number of sound effects or actions for the children to participate in. Rather than expecting them to remember the actions, you may want to prompt the children at the appropriate point in the story, as suggested below. You may also find it helpful to show the children some simple illustrations for each part of the story.

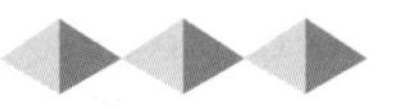

Do you remember, last week, we heard about baby Moses, who was found in the river by a princess and was looked after in the royal palace in Egypt? God was looking after Moses, and when Moses grew up, God gave him a special job to do.

God's people had been in Egypt for a very long time and were being very badly treated by Pharaoh. God wanted his people to be free again, so he sent Moses to speak to Pharaoh and tell him to let God's people go. But Pharaoh wouldn't listen: he just said 'No!'

Encourage the children to shake their heads and say 'No!'

So God made ten really bad things happen, to try to change Pharaoh's mind. There was no clean water to drink *(ask the children to mime drinking from a cup)*. There were jumping frogs *(jump up and down, saying, 'Ribbit, ribbit')* and nasty creepy-crawlies *(mime swatting a fly)*. Then the animals got sick *(encourage sad mooing)*, and so did the people *(look very sad)*. There was hail and thunder *(encourage claps of thunder)* and the sky became very dark *(put your hands over your eyes)*. But Pharaoh still said 'No!'

Encourage the children to join in, saying 'No!'

Then God had to send a very sad day, when one person in every Egyptian family died—but God looked after his people and kept them safe. Pharaoh had had enough, so he sent Moses and all God's people out of Egypt. They were free!

Encourage the children to cheer.

The people had to leave Egypt very quickly and they couldn't take much with them. They hadn't gone very far when Pharaoh changed his mind. Pharaoh and his army chased God's people all the way to the edge of the sea. God's people were worried that they were stuck, but God was still in control. He made the sea split in half so that Moses and all the people could go right through the middle of the sea.

Pharaoh and his army chased them into the sea, but God hadn't finished yet. He wouldn't let anything bad happen to his people, so he made the sea come crashing back over the top of the Egyptian army.

Moses and the rest of God's people were finally free *(encourage more cheering)*. They had a very long journey ahead of them, but God would be with them, every step of the way.

Prayer

Thank you, God, for setting your people free and for being with them every step of their long journey. Thank you that you are with us too, wherever we go, every step of the way. Amen.

Songs

Songs today could include:

- How did Moses cross the Red Sea? (Hugh Mitchell and J.C. Brumfield)

Take home

You could suggest that your families play some chasing games this week and talk about what happened in today's story.

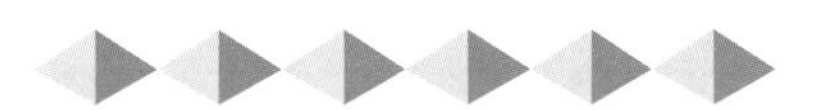

God's special rules

For the team

Refer to pages 6–8 to see how the activity areas work together

Session theme

This is the final session exploring the life of Moses, focusing today on the ten commandments and the need for God's people to live life God's way. Rather than expecting children to try to remember all of the rules, this session focuses on the reason why God gives us rules and what it means to love and respect God and other people.

Bible text: Exodus 19—20

Team prayer

Heavenly Father, you created these rules for us to live by because you have a great plan for our lives and want us to live life in the best way possible. Help us to share this message today with the children and families that we meet.

Activity areas

Sensory, tactile, malleable

Provide air-hardening clay, along with small tools including rolling-pins and pointed tools for mark-making. Give each child a fist-sized piece of clay and encourage them to roll it out to make a small tablet, before writing or drawing into the slab of clay. Children could write letters or words that are important to them, the numbers 1–10, or simple shapes or images.

Talk about how God's rules were written on two large slabs of stone for the people to carry with them.

Small world play

Provide a selection of pebbles, along with smaller gravel pieces, for the children to use to build mountains within the play area. Use the play figures to re-enact climbing the mountains.

Talk about children's own experiences of walking up a hill or perhaps seeing a mountain while on holiday. Explain that the mountain in today's story was much higher than any mountains in this country.

Role play / dressing up

Set up a tent or help the children to build their own from a selection of sheets and blankets, chairs and laundry dryers. Supervise the process to ensure that the finished tent is secure enough for children to role-play camping in it. You could also provide a selection of camping paraphernalia, such as sleeping bags, stools and cooking equipment.

Talk about how the Israelites spent many years travelling around in the wilderness after they were freed from Egypt. They would not have had all the camping equipment that we might have.

Creative

Provide some pieces of card, along with a selection of letter and number stamps, with ink pads or paint. Encourage children and carers to explore different letter or number forms.

Talk about numbers and letters that are familiar to the children. Explain that God wrote his special rules down so that everybody could see them and remember them.

Construction

Provide large cushions, pillows, beanbags and duvets and ask the children and carers to heap them on top of each other to create a mountain. Throw a grey sheet or blanket over the top and, if it is safe to do so, invite the children to climb up the mountain, one child at a time, under supervision. If the mountain starts to collapse, reconstruct it before allowing other children to have a turn.

Talk about how Moses climbed Mount Sinai on his own, where he met God and was given the special rules.

Books

Reintroduce the story books about Moses that you offered last week, along with children's Bibles and a selection of non-fiction picture books about mountains and counting books.

Share these books with the children, offering to read the stories to children if they so wish and talking about the illustrations in the books.

Sand

Provide scoops and spades and invite children and carers to work together to scoop the sand into a sand mountain, in the middle of the sand tray. Encourage the children to experiment with both wet and dry sand to see which makes a better mountain.

Talk about children's own experiences of mountains to find out whether anyone has seen or even been up a mountain. How did they travel up the mountain? Explain that Moses would have walked or climbed to the top of Mount Sinai.

Puzzles, toys, games

Among the toys and games offered today, provide a selection of age-appropriate board games with simple rules that the children can follow.

Snack time

Story time

The story for today's session allows the children to add some sound effects, as in the previous session. This story involves sharing the ten commandments, which are repeated to help the children to remember them. Invite the children and carers to sit on the floor with you, ready to join in as you share the story.

Do you remember that we heard last week about God's people being set free from Egypt? God planned for them to live a happy new life in a beautiful place, but God's people weren't ready. They spent all their time moaning and groaning *(encourage children to add appropriate sound effects).*

God decided to give his people some rules to follow so that they could all enjoy their new life and freedom, to help them to take care of each other, and to live lives that would make God happy.

Moses climbed up, up, up a very tall mountain.

Encourage the children to pretend to climb up a mountain.

At the top of the mountain, God told Moses his special rules.

As you go through the rules below, demonstrate how to count them out on both hands, and encourage the children to do the same. Periodically run through the rules to recap them, encouraging the children to repeat them with you. If appropriate, explain the rules to the children in more detail, without spending too much time on any single one.

Number 1: Always remember that I am your God and I love you very much.

Number 2: Don't treat anything else as if it's as important as me.

Number 3: My name is special, so don't use it badly.

Number 4: Work for six days, then take a rest day, just like I did when I created the world.

Number 5: Respect your mum and dad; listen to them and be kind.

Number 6: Do not kill anyone.

Number 7: When you get married, respect your husband or wife and look after them.

Number 8: Don't take anything that belongs to someone else.

Number 9: Be honest; don't tell lies.

Number 10: Respect what other people have and don't just wish you had everything.

God wrote the rules on two big blocks of stone to help the people remember them. Many, many years later, Jesus helped people to understand these rules by telling them to remember just two rules: love God and love other people. If we do these two things, then we keep God's ten special rules.

Prayer

Dear God, thank you that you gave your people ten special rules to help them to live life in the best way. Help us to follow these rules, and help us to love you and love other people. Amen

Songs

Songs today could include:

- I can do all things (Jim Bailey)
- If I've been wrong (Sammy Horner)

Take home

Suggest that your families might find it helpful to think about a list of family rules that they want to try to follow. Encourage them to talk about why rules are important to keep everybody safe and well.

10

Joshua and the walls of Jericho

Refer to pages 6–8 to see how the activity areas work together

For the team

Session theme

As we explore the story of Joshua today, we are reminded that there is nothing God cannot do and that when God speaks to us, we need to trust him by doing the things that he says, just as Joshua did.

Bible text: Joshua 6

Team prayer

Heavenly Father, sometimes we face situations that seem difficult, even impossible. Today's story reminds us that nothing is impossible for you. Help us to trust you in every circumstance.

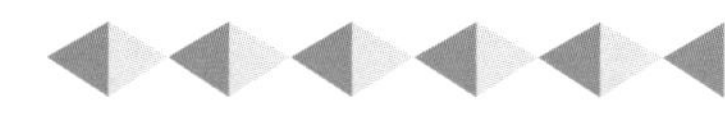

Activity areas

Small world play

Provide a small toy castle (or make one using a sturdy cardboard box), along with appropriate play characters such as knights or soldiers. Encourage children and carers to play as though they are defending or attacking the castle, using the appropriate tools.

Talk about the way that they would attack a castle. Explain that the walls of Jericho were a bit like a castle, but Joshua and his men had none of these weapons when they came to Jericho. God made it possible to enter the city without them.

Role play / dressing up

Create an area where children can pretend to be a marching band. Provide appropriate costumes, such as soldiers' uniforms or tabards and hats, and a range of musical instruments, including drums and blowers.

Talk about how soldiers in a marching band keep in time together and how they play their music at the same time as marching together. Explain that Joshua and his men had to march around the city walls, playing their trumpets just as God told them.

Creative

Provide thick coloured A4 paper, along with colouring pens and pencils and stickers. Invite the children to decorate their sheet of paper as they wish, before rolling it into a cone to make a 'trumpet'. Help children to fix the cone together using a small piece of sticky tape.

Talk about how brass players really play a trumpet and how noisy these instruments can be.

Construction

Gather a large collection of cardboard boxes and work together to build the walls of Jericho in a square or rectangular shape. This construction will be used in the storytelling today.

Talk about how large the city walls of Jericho would have been, and how, being made of rock or stone, they would have been far sturdier than these cardboard walls.

Books

Along with children's Bibles and books that retell the story of Joshua, provide a selection of picture books about castles, knights, musical instruments and bands.

Encourage children to look at the pictures of Jericho in the children's Bibles and the pictures of castles in the picture books. Ask them what similarities and differences they notice.

Water

Provide some water pistols or squirters and invite the children to use them to knock down paper cups, which you can place on the edge of the water tray.

Talk about how Joshua and the army had no weapons to use to knock down the city walls. God destroyed the city, though, when the army followed his instructions.

Sand

Ensure that the sand is wet enough to build with, and provide a selection of buckets, spades and plastic cups. Help the children to build a large sandcastle in the sandpit before inviting them to demolish it.

As they build, talk about the features of the castle, using appropriate vocabulary. Talk about how easy it is to demolish a castle made of sand and how difficult it would be if it were really made of stone.

Puzzles, toys, games

Among the toys offered today, try to include a selection of building bricks or blocks so that children can build their own walls.

Snack time

Story time

This story will take place, dramatically, around the cardboard city created in the construction area. Before the story begins, position four helpers at the corners of your city, ready to demolish the walls at the appropriate point. Invite children to participate in the story by playing the parts of Joshua, an angel, seven priests (holding the trumpets created earlier in the session), and an army, who need no props. The children may need prompting at the appropriate moments in the story.

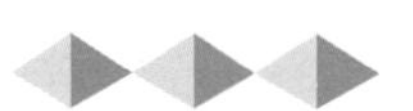

After they left Egypt, God's people spent a very long time wandering around in the desert, learning how to follow God's special rules. Eventually, the time came when they were ready to find the new home that God had promised to them.

One day, when Joshua and the rest of God's people were close to the city of Jericho, an angel appeared to Joshua.

Invite the appropriate children to stand together and pretend to talk.

The angel told Joshua that God wanted the people to go into the city of Jericho, where his enemies lived. The angel told Joshua that God would be with them, but they would have to do exactly as God said.

Joshua shared God's plan with all the people and they did exactly what they were told. First, all God's people marched around the city walls every day for six days, while the seven priests blew on their trumpets.

Encourage all the children to march around the walls, while the seven volunteers make a noise with their trumpets. Count six times around the city.

After that, on the seventh day, everyone marched very quietly around the walls.

Encourage the children to do this.

When they had been all the way round, the priests had to blow very hard on their trumpets, and all the people had to shout and make a very loud noise.

Give the children a cue when to begin and when to stop making a noise.

Suddenly, the walls of the city crashed down.

Ensure that the four helpers have had advance warning and are ready to topple the walls. After the excitement has subsided, invite the children to sit around the destroyed walls as you finish the story.

God is more powerful than walls made of stone, or armies of soldiers. Because Joshua and the people did what God told them to do, the walls of Jericho came crashing down.

Prayer

Dear God, thank you that you are so strong and powerful. Please help us to do the things you tell us to do, just like Joshua. Amen

Songs

Songs today could include:

- Joshua at Jericho (Ian Smale)
- The following adaptation of 'Here we go round the mulberry bush' by Sharon Broome:

Here we go round the Jericho wall,
Jericho wall, Jericho wall.
Here we go round the Jericho wall,
early in the morning.

This is the way we blow our horns,
blow our horns, blow our horns.
This is the way we blow our horns,
early in the morning.

This is the way we quietly walk,
quietly walk, quietly walk.
This is the way we quietly walk,
early in the morning.

This is the way we shout really loud,
shout really loud, shout really loud.
This is the way we shout really loud,
early in the morning.

This is the way the walls fall down,
walls fall down, walls fall down.
This is the way the walls fall down,
early in the morning.

Take home

Suggest to your families that they may like to visit a castle or large historic walls this week. Encourage them to explore how wide, how high and how strong those walls are. Can they imagine the walls of Jericho crashing down?

11

Ruth: someone who cared

For the team

Refer to pages 6–8 to see how the activity areas work together

Session theme

During this session, we explore the story of Ruth and the choice that she made to take care of Naomi. Through today's story, we share what it means to be people who care for others, and we reflect on the way that God cares for us.

Bible text: Ruth 1—4

Team prayer

Father God, thank you that you care for all people. Help us today to find ways to care for the children and their families and to encourage them to care for other people too.

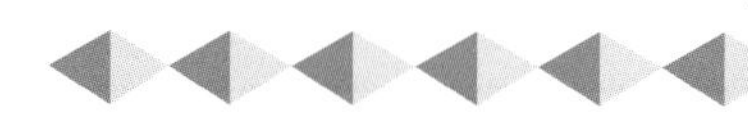

Activity areas

Sensory, tactile, malleable

Roll out small pieces of air-drying clay with a rolling pin, and provide a selection of different seeds and grains for children to press into their clay plaques. Red clay can offer a more aesthetically pleasing finish than grey clay for this activity.

Talk about the different shapes, sizes, colours and patterns that children notice in the seeds and grains. Explain that Ruth was very poor when she arrived in Bethlehem, so she went to the fields to gather up the grain that was left behind from the harvest.

Small world play

Set up a farm scene, with fields, tractors, combine harvesters and hay bales, along with people figurines to act as farm workers. Help the children to re-enact harvesting the crops in the fields.

Talk about the farm vehicles and the way in which they are used to harvest crops nowadays. Explain that in the time of Ruth, farm workers would have gathered in the crops by hand.

Role play / dressing up

Provide a selection of ride-on tractors and trailers, along with a selection of toy tools, such as spades, rakes, watering cans and so on. Encourage the children to play the roles of farmers, taking care of the crops that they are growing.

Talk about the way that Ruth found work on a farm. The farmer there was a kind man who took care of her, giving her a chance to find plenty of food.

Creative

Provide large sheets of paper, paintbrushes and poster paints in a variety of colours, and invite children to come and paint a portrait of their family.

Talk about the different people that children choose to include as members of their family. Ruth looked after her mother-in-law.

Books

Provide a selection of books about family, food and farming, along with children's Bibles and other story books about Ruth and Naomi.

Share the books with the children, reading the stories as they wish. You could talk about the differences between farming as it is seen in the books and farming at the time of Ruth, comparing the illustrations in the books.

Water

Gather a few 'families' of bath toys, such as bath ducks and fish, and add them to the water tray for the children to play with, matching the family members together.

Talk about the way that families take care of each other, just as Ruth took care of Naomi, and Boaz took care of Ruth.

Sand

Replace the sand in the tray with grain, such as barley, wheat, oats or corn. Encourage the children to handle the grain, letting it flow through their fingers, as well as using sand tools, including a selection of spoons, scoops and sieves. You could also show the children how to grind the grain with a pestle and mortar.

Talk about the way that we still use these different grains in our food today, just as people did in Ruth's day.

Puzzles, toys, games

You could reinforce the themes of farming and caring for others by providing a selection of farm-themed toys, games and puzzles as well as resources with a 'people who care for us' theme, such as doctors, vets, teachers and so on.

Snack time

Story time

For today's storytelling, you will need a number of people figurines. These could be play people, but it may be more effective if you prepare a number of paper or felt silhouette figures (three women and four men), each in a different colour.

Begin by placing three of the women and three of the men together, as three couples, on the floor to one side of the scene, with the children sitting around in a circle. You could use different coloured pieces of paper or fabric as backgrounds to the scene. Point to the appropriate figures as you tell the story.

There was once a woman called Naomi who lived with her husband, her two sons and their two wives. Sadly, Naomi's husband and her two sons both died *(remove the men from the scene)*, leaving Naomi and both her daughters-in-law, who were called Orpah and Ruth.

Naomi told Orpah and Ruth that they could go back to their own families, and this is what Orpah decided to do *(remove one woman from the scene)*, but Ruth stayed with Naomi. She wanted to look after Naomi. God was looking after them both, too.

Naomi and Ruth travelled back to the town that Naomi had come from *(move the silhouettes to the other side of the scene)*. Ruth knew she would have to find work to help to look after Naomi, so she worked on a farm, picking up the leftover grains to make food for them both. Ruth worked hard to look after Naomi. God was looking after them both, too.

The owner of the farm was a man called Boaz. He saw the way that Ruth helped to look after Naomi. He wanted to help Ruth, so he made sure that there was always enough food left for her to collect. Boaz looked after Ruth, and God was looking after them all, too.

Boaz wanted to do more to care for Ruth and Naomi, so he asked Ruth to marry him, and she said 'Yes'. Naomi was so happy that Boaz was going to look after Ruth. God was looking after them, too.

Ruth and Boaz had a baby son and their family grew and grew. Ruth looked after her baby and Naomi. Boaz looked after Ruth. God looked after them all, and he looks after us, too.

Prayer

Dear God, thank you that you care for us, just as you cared for Ruth, Naomi and Boaz. Help us to find ways of showing this care and love for other people, too. Amen

Songs

Songs today could include:

- Big family of God (Becky Drake)

Take home

Encourage your families to talk about the ways that they care for each other, as they get on with their normal lives, and to look for ways to care for other people too.

12

Samuel: a boy who listened

For the team

Refer to pages 6–8 to see how the activity areas work together

Session theme

This session tells the story of Samuel and the way that he heard God's voice even when he was very young. This apparently simple story speaks of an extraordinary truth: God speaks directly to his people. It also speaks an important truth to the children who come to the session: God is not just for the grown-ups, but for children too.

Bible text: 1 Samuel 3

Team prayer

Father God, as we speak to you, you hear our prayers. Help us to listen to you too, to hear the things that you want to share with us and with the children we meet today.

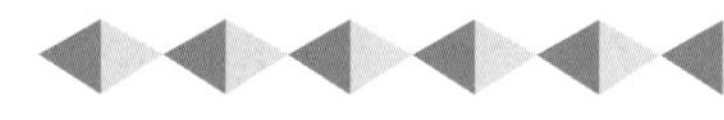

Activity areas

Sensory, tactile, malleable

Prepare a sound lotto game, with playing cards showing symbols of well-known sound sources, such as a ringing phone, doorbell, fire engine and so on. You will also need sound clips to play, which can be sourced online, and counters with which the children can cover the appropriate image on their playing card when the related sound is played.

Talk about how we need to listen carefully to hear the different sounds, just as Samuel had to listen carefully to hear what God had to say to him.

Small world play

Provide a dolls' house, including a child's bedroom and an adult's bedroom, and a selection of people figurines. Encourage the children to play out a bedroom routine for the children in the dolls' house.

Talk about the way that God spoke to Samuel when he was in bed. Samuel kept going to Eli's room to ask him what he wanted, but it wasn't Eli calling—it was God.

Role play / dressing up

Create a bedroom scene, using a play mat, blankets or sleeping bags and pillows to create beds or cots. Add some books to use for bedtime stories and soft toys for cuddles.

Talk about the routines that children follow before they go to bed—getting washed and undressed, perhaps hearing a story and saying a prayer. Tell the children that it was when Samuel had gone to bed that he heard God's voice calling him.

Creative

Provide strips of card that will fit around the children's heads and a supply of coloured card, with which you can make two ears to attach to the band. The ears could be human or distinctive animal ear shapes, such as elephant, rabbit or cat. Wrap the card strips round the children's heads and secure with sticky tape.

Talk about the different shapes of the ears and the way that all animals use their ears to listen for sounds.

Construction

Provide a selection of small cardboard boxes and tubes for the children to use to build a model of the temple where Eli and Samuel lived. You could also provide some catalogues and invite the children to cut out pictures of appropriate furniture to add to the rooms, such as a bed for Samuel.

Talk about the fact that Eli and Samuel lived in the temple rather than a house like ours.

Books

Display a selection of books about Samuel and children's Bibles so that the children can find out more about today's story, as well as children's books of prayers. You could also provide some story books about going to bed.

Read the books to the children, as they wish. Share the prayers with the children and explain that when we pray, we are talking to God, who also talks to us when we listen to him.

Water

Provide a selection of objects of different weights for the children to drop into the water. Encourage them to listen to the splash as each object enters the water.

Talk about how we have to listen really carefully to the light objects that make a quiet splash, while the heavier objects create much louder sounds.

Puzzles, toys, games

Alongside the toys and puzzles provided today, you could organise a few listening games for the children to play together. They could include Grandma's Footsteps, Chinese Whispers and Simon Says.

Snack time

Story time

Explain that everybody is going to get involved and play a role in today's story. Tell any adult carers that they will play the part of Eli, the priest who lived at the temple, and all the children will play the part of Samuel, who was looked after by Eli. Explain that, as you tell the story, each of the 'Samuels' will need to go and find an 'Eli' at the appropriate point.

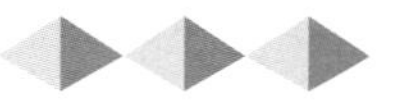

Samuel was a very special boy. His mummy, Hannah, had prayed very hard for God to give her a baby, and God had done just that. Hannah knew that Samuel would have a special job to do for God, so she asked Eli, the priest, to take care of him in the temple and teach him all about God. Samuel loved learning more and more about God.

One night, when Samuel and Eli were asleep in their bedrooms, Samuel heard a voice calling his name: 'Samuel, Samuel.'

Samuel thought it was Eli calling him, so he went to find him *(prompt the children to go and 'wake up' their Eli)*. But Eli was fast asleep. He yawned and he stretched *(encourage the adults to respond appropriately)* and told Samuel that he hadn't called him. 'Go back to bed, Samuel,' Eli said kindly.

Samuel went back to bed, but it wasn't long before the same thing happened again. Samuel ran through to Eli *(prompt the children as necessary)*, but Eli was asleep. He yawned and he stretched *(prompt the adults if necessary)* and told Samuel that he hadn't called him. 'Go back to bed, Samuel,' Eli said again.

Samuel went back to bed again, and one more time he heard a voice calling his name: 'Samuel, Samuel.' Samuel ran back to Eli yet again *(prompt the children)*, but Eli was asleep. He yawned and he stretched *(prompt the adults)* and he scratched his head.

Then he said to Samuel, 'It isn't me calling you, Samuel, but I think I know who it is. God is calling you; I think he has something to say to you. The next time you hear God calling your name, you need to say, "I am listening, God," and then listen carefully to what he says.'

So Samuel went back to bed, and the next time he heard his name being called, he knew it was God speaking to him. 'I am listening,' he said to God, and he listened very carefully to everything that God told him—not just that night, but for the rest of his life.

Prayer

Thank you, God, that when we speak to you, you listen and you speak to us too. Please help us to listen to you, just as Samuel did. Amen

Songs

Songs today could include:

- On my bed (Ian Smale)
- You need to natter to God (Doug Horley)

Take home

Encourage your families to take some time to pray together this week, not just speaking to God but listening to him too. You may want to offer more advice to your families about this, as appropriate.

13

David and Goliath

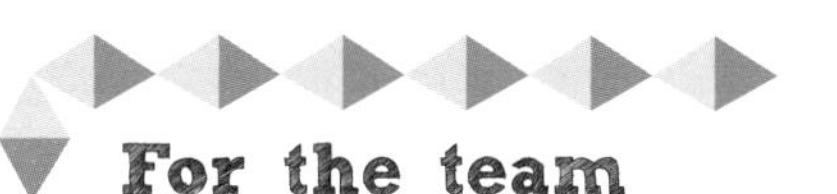

For the team

Refer to pages 6–8 to see how the activity areas work together

Session theme

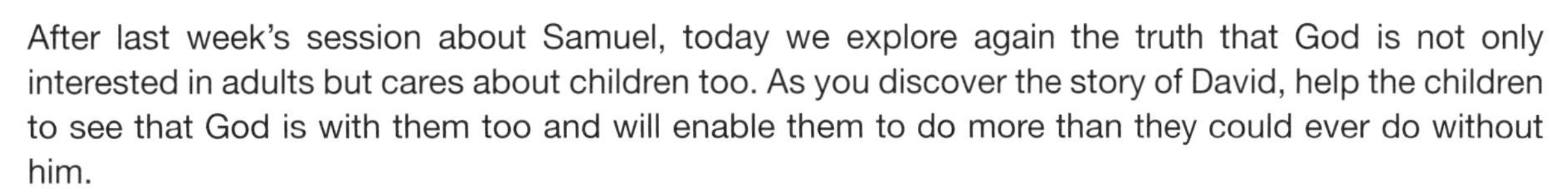

After last week's session about Samuel, today we explore again the truth that God is not only interested in adults but cares about children too. As you discover the story of David, help the children to see that God is with them too and will enable them to do more than they could ever do without him.

Bible text: 1 Samuel 17

Team prayer

Almighty God, there is nothing too big or too difficult for you, and yet you choose to involve us in your great plans. Help us to remember that with your power at work within us, we can do much more than we could ever imagine.

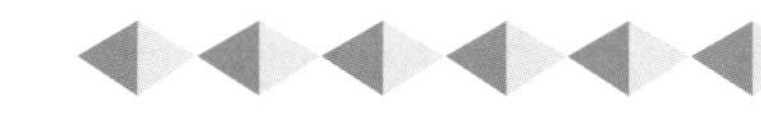

Activity areas

Small world play

Create a countryside or field scene with sheep figures, along with a shepherd. You could also include figures of a wolf, bear and lion and encourage the children to re-enact the way that the shepherd would protect his sheep from other animals that came to attack them.

Talk about how David cared for his father's sheep, protecting them from wild animals, before he had to go to the battle scene.

Role play / dressing up

Provide a selection of items, such as breastplates, shields and helmets, that can be used as armour for children to wear.

Talk about how David tried on King Saul's own armour, but, because it was all too big for him, David went to fight Goliath wearing only his ordinary clothes.

Creative

Gather some smooth pebbles and provide paints and stickers for children to use to decorate a pebble. Acrylic paints work particularly well, but children will need to wear aprons to protect their clothes.

Talk about the way that David used a small pebble to defeat Goliath. When we trust God, he can do amazing things through us that we cannot do on our own.

Construction

Provide some large cardboard boxes and help the children and carers to build a tall tower with them. Invite the children to come and stand next to the tower to see how small they are in comparison to it.

Talk about how tall Goliath was, compared to David—just as the children are very small when compared to the tall tower.

Books

Along with children's Bibles and story books about David and Goliath, you could also provide a selection of stories that show the world through the eyes of a small child, focusing on how it feels to be the youngest or the smallest. You could also include non-fiction books that explore the concepts of size comparison and ordering.

Share the books with the children, reading aloud as they wish, and discussing how they feel about being the youngest or the smallest in their family.

Water

Place an assortment of pebbles and some clean gravel in the bottom of the water tray. Invite the children to scoop five smooth stones out of the water, from amid the gravel, counting them as they do so.

Talk about the different stones as the children choose them. Ask the children why they think David chose the stones that he found in the stream.

Sand

Fill the tray with wet sand that can be used to build sandcastles with buckets and spades. Encourage the children to demolish the sandcastles, once they have built them, crushing them under their hands or feet.

Talk about the way that David toppled Goliath with God's help.

Puzzles, toys, games

Among the toys offered today, provide a selection of different stacking cups and cubes for children to use to build tall towers.

Snack time

Story time

Invite one of your shortest members to play the part of David, along with one of your tallest adults to play Goliath, and another adult to play King Saul. Divide the rest of the group into two halves and ask them to sit facing each other. You will need a few props—a crown for Saul, a couple of items of armour from the dressing-up area (which will need to be too big for the child involved) and a catapult.

God's people were in trouble. A mean and scary army was trying to attack them and they didn't know what to do.

Encourage the families sitting on Goliath's side to growl or roar in a menacing way.

King Saul didn't know what to do, either. Every day, Goliath, the giant, would come out and shout to God's people, 'Who will come and fight me?' God's people were scared *(encourage the families sitting with David to tremble and murmur)*. They had forgotten that God was with them and would help them.

One day, a young boy called David was sent to the battlefield to take some food to his big brothers. He was very surprised when he saw how frightened God's people were. Then he saw Goliath and heard him shout, 'Who will come and fight me?'

David wasn't afraid. He knew that God was with him. He told King Saul that he would fight Goliath. King Saul was very surprised by this—he didn't think a young boy should fight against a giant—but David told Saul that he could, because God was with him. King Saul tried to give David some of his armour to keep him safe, but it was all too big, so David took the armour off. He knew that he would be OK because he knew that God was with him.

David went down to the stream and found five smooth stones. He took out his little slingshot, put the first stone into it and catapulted the stone up into the air. The stone flew straight to Goliath's head, knocked him down and killed him.

David killed Goliath, not by being big and strong, not by being brave and clever, but by trusting God to help him.

Prayer

Dear God, thank you that we do not need to be afraid of anything, because you are always with us. Even though we might feel quite small, we can do anything if we trust in you, just as David did. Amen

Songs

Songs today could include:

- I once was frightened of spiders (Ian Smale)
- My God is so big, so strong and so mighty (Anon)

Take home

Suggest that your families might like to create a height chart in their homes, where they can measure each member of their family and compare their heights. Remind your families that God's love for us is not dependent upon height or age; he loves us all the same.

14 David and Jonathan

For the team

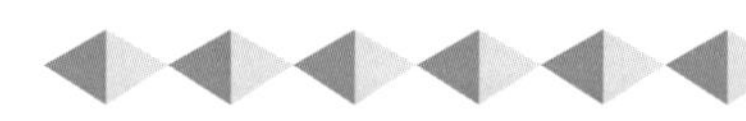

Refer to pages 6–8 to see how the activity areas work together

Session theme

This is the second of three sessions that explore the life of David. Today we find out about his friendship with Jonathan and the way that God kept David safe, even when he was in danger. Through the session we focus on the gift of friendship.

Bible text: 1 Samuel 18—20

Team prayer

Dear God, thank you that you place us within communities, to be loved and cared for by others. Please help us to demonstrate true friendship to those who come to our group, not only today but in all of life's circumstances.

Activity areas

Sensory, tactile, malleable

Before the session, make some copies of the play dough mat face template on page 124 and laminate them so that children can use them, together with the play dough provided, to create an image of one of their friends.

Talk about friends and why they are important to us. Explain that today we will be talking about the friendship between David and Jonathan and why they were important to each other.

Small world play

Provide a toy castle, along with appropriately related figures, such as knights, princes and princesses, for the children to use to explore life in a castle.

Talk about how David went to live with King Saul and his family in the royal palace. It would have been very different from life as a shepherd, taking care of the sheep.

Role play / dressing up

Provide a selection of royalty-themed dressing-up outfits, such as cloaks and crowns, princess dresses and tiaras. You could also set up a special chair as a throne.

Talk about what the children would do if they were the king or queen. King Saul became a bad king who stopped listening to God. What would you need to do to be a good king or queen?

Creative

Provide some short lengths of wool, cord or ribbon and a selection of brightly coloured beads or short lengths of drinking straws. Invite the children and carers to create a friendship bracelet with the beads, not to keep for themselves but to give to one of their friends as a present.

Talk about how David and Jonathan were really good friends who cared about each other, and discuss the way we care about our friends too. Talk about the children's friends. What makes those people special?

Construction

Provide a selection of really large cardboard boxes and make caves by cutting a hole out of the front of each one. You could develop this activity by making the box more cave-like, perhaps adding texture with papier mâché or simply painting it grey.

Talk about how David had to hide from King Saul in a cave, which was where he could meet Jonathan. What sort of places do we like to hide in, perhaps when we're playing Hide and Seek?

Books

Alongside children's Bibles and books about David and his life, you could offer a selection of books about families, friendship and feelings.

Offer to read or share the books with the children, as they wish, and talk about the issues that are raised in them. Talk about the children's own experiences as well as David's story.

Sand

Create some cards with images of well-known pairs, appropriate to the interests of your children. They could include well-known characters from cartoons, stories or nursery rhymes. Bury the cards in the sand for the children to uncover and match the friends together.

Talk about how David and Jonathan are well known for their friendship, in the same way that these characters are known to 'belong together'.

Puzzles, toys, games

Alongside the toys and puzzles that you set up for the children to play with today, you could also organise a game of Hide and Seek or other hiding games.

Snack time

Story time

You will need some volunteers, perhaps members of your team, to help with today's story. You will need someone to play the part of Saul, who can be seated on a throne and wear a crown, a second volunteer to play the part of David, and a third to be Jonathan. Encourage the volunteers to respond to the storytelling, displaying the appropriate emotions and actions at the right points in the script, as you narrate.

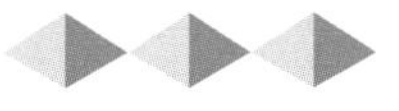

Do you remember, last time, we heard the story of David and how he killed the giant Goliath by trusting God to help him? After this had happened, David went to live with the king, Saul. At first, Saul was pleased to have David in his home. He was very proud of the way that David had defeated Goliath, and he liked to have David in his team. Saul introduced David to his son, Jonathan, and they became very good friends. Everyone was happy.

But over time, Saul changed his mind. He was jealous of David and all the things that he could do. David was a good soldier, better at fighting than Saul. He was a good musician, better at playing instruments than Saul, and he was good and kind, much kinder than Saul. King Saul decided that he didn't want David to be around any more, so he came up with a plan to kill David, all because he was jealous!

Jonathan was very worried about his friend, so he made a very difficult choice. He decided he would help David to escape and get away from his dad, and help David find a place where he could be safe.

King Saul was very angry with David and with Jonathan. How could his own son help his enemy? But God was taking care of David. For many years, Saul chased David, but David never hurt Saul, even though Saul tried many times to hurt David.

David trusted God and did the things that God told him to, and God took care of David. One day it was David's turn to become king. He always remembered his friend, Jonathan, and the way that he had helped him.

Prayer

Dear God, thank you for our friends and for the fun things we do together. Please help us to be good friends, just as Jonathan was a good friend to David. Amen

Songs

Songs today could include:

- I once was frightened of spiders (Ian Smale)
- Our God is a great big God (Nigel and Jo Hemming)

Take home

Encourage the children to take the friendship bracelets that they have made to give to one of their friends this week, as a sign that they care.

15

King David praises God

For the team

Refer to pages 6–8 to see how the activity areas work together

Session theme

This is the final one of three sessions about the life of David. In today's session, we explore the way that David honoured God through his singing and dancing and in preparing to build the temple.

Bible text: 1 Chronicles 17 and 22—29

Team prayer

Almighty God, you are worthy of all our praises. Today we celebrate all your great gifts as we bring our praises to you.

Activity areas

Sensory, tactile, malleable

Prepare some play dough, perhaps coloured yellow or 'gold' with food colouring and sprinkled with glitter to make it sparkle. Provide a selection of sequins and acrylic gems for children to use to create a play dough plaque.

Talk about the way that King David gathered together gold, silver, gems and precious stones to be used in decorating the temple.

Role play / dressing up

Provide a selection of musical instruments, including percussion instruments and any others you have available that children can use safely. You could also provide small flags and streamers for the children to dance with in this area.

Talk about how David used the music that he played, and his dancing, to show God how much he loved him. We can show God we love him when we dance and sing too.

Creative

Gather a selection of clean, used, small plastic bottles and provide different grains and pulses, such as rice, dried beans, split peas and lentils. Help the children to pour a selection of grains and pulses into a bottle, using a scoop and funnel, before tightening the lid securely to create a shaker. Children could then use small stickers to decorate their shakers.

Talk about how David used music to show God how much he loved him. We can do the same, perhaps by shaking our shakers when we sing songs to God.

Construction

Provide a selection of building blocks and invite the children and carers to use them to create the most spectacular building they can imagine.

Talk about how David planned to build a very special temple for God, to show how great he thought God was. In the end, though, it was his son Solomon who built the temple.

Books

Gather a selection of children's Bibles and books about the life of David, as well as children's books of psalms, and books about music and dancing.

Read to the children, as they wish, and talk about the things that they find interesting. Explain that David wrote many of the psalms that we find in the Bible.

Water

Provide a few plastic plates and cups, washing-up liquid, cloths, sponges and tea towels for the children to use to pretend to wash up.

Talk about how David gave everyone different jobs to do, to contribute towards building the temple, just as we can have jobs to do at home to help our parents.

Sand

Bury some shiny costume jewellery, large beads, coins and sparkles in the sand and provide sand tools for children to use to hunt for the treasure.

Talk about how David asked people to gather together the gold and precious gems to be used to build a special temple for God.

Puzzles, toys, games

You could play some musical games today, such as Musical Bumps or Musical Statues, to remind the children of David's love of music.

Snack time

Story time

Before you begin today's story, ask the children to gather the following props to hold in their laps, ready to bring up at the appropriate point. You will need a variety of percussion instruments, pebbles, sticks, costume jewellery and 'gems', from the activities you have offered today.

Do you remember what we have found out about David during the last two sessions? When he was just a young boy, he killed the giant, Goliath; then he went to live with the king, Saul. But Saul was jealous of David and all the things he could do, so his son Jonathan helped David to escape. God kept David safe for many years, until David became the king.

When David was king, he decided to do something to show God how special he is. He drew some plans to build a new temple; then he told the people what they needed to bring.

Prompt the children to bring the things they are holding, as you mention them in the story, and make a pile in front of you.

'We need stones and wood,' said David, and the people brought great big stones and the best wood they could find.

'Iron, bronze, silver and gold,' said David, and the people brought the precious metals that they needed.

'Precious jewels,' said David, and the people brought shiny, beautiful jewels too.

David didn't build the temple; his son would do that job. But when all the things they needed were gathered together, David led the people in singing songs and playing instruments, all to worship God and tell him just how great he is.

Prayer

God, you are an amazing God, more precious than jewels. Thank you for everything that you do for us. Amen

Songs

Songs today could include:

- Shake my shaker (Nigel Hemming)
- What noise shall we make? (Lucy East)

Take home

You could invite your families to join you for a church service, if appropriate, or consider offering a special toddler service in the week ahead.

16

Elijah and the fire

For the team

Refer to pages 6–8 to see how the activity areas work together

Session theme

During this session we explore one episode from Elijah's life, when he confronted Ahab and proved that God is the true God. Through this session, we will show the children that God has power over all things.

Bible text: 1 Kings 18

Team prayer

Almighty God, we remember that you are all-powerful. Help us to share this message with the children who come to our group today.

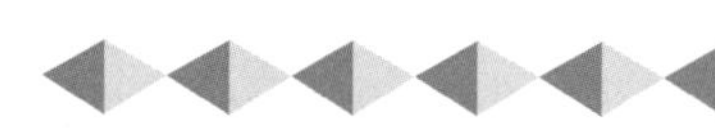

Activity areas

Sensory, tactile, malleable

Copy the play dough mat template with the picture of the empty altars on page 125, and laminate the copies in preparation for the session. Provide play dough in fiery colours—red, orange and yellow—and invite the children and carers to create flames from it, to stick above Elijah's altar.

Talk about how God sent the fire on to the altar when Elijah prayed, to show the people that he was the real God.

Small world play

Provide toy fire engines and fire fighters, perhaps with a road play mat so that the children can pretend to chase through the streets to put out fires. You could also provide a dolls' house for children to practise taking a fire escape route out of a house.

Talk about how fire fighters use water to put fires out. In today's story, we will hear about a time when God sent a fire from heaven that burnt everything on the altar, even though water had already been poured all over it.

Role play / dressing up

Create a fire station scene where children can dress up as fire fighters. Let them use a play phone to practise taking an emergency call, 'writing' the messages that they take.

Talk about how fire fighters are there to keep us safe in an emergency, although we should never do anything dangerous that could cause a problem. Talk about what we should do if we ever see a fire and how we should act to stay safe.

Construction

Work with the children and carers to build a model of the altar, like the one Elijah built in the story. You will need twelve large stones, but make sure that they are not too heavy for the children to carry themselves. Alternatively, you could stuff twelve large brown paper bags or black plastic sacks for children to use as stones.

Talk about how, at the time of Elijah, people had to build altars to offer sacrifices or gifts to God. We do not have to do that now, because Jesus came to make things right between us and God.

Books

Provide a selection of books about fires, fire engines and fire fighters, along with children's Bibles and story books about Elijah, which could include other episodes from his life.

Share the books with the children who ask to have them read to them, and talk about the things that are of interest to the children.

Water

Provide water squirters and pistols so that children can pretend to be fire fighters, putting out a fire with the water.

Talk about how we use water to put fires out—but even though everything had been covered in water, God is so powerful that his fire still burnt everything on the altar.

Sand

Help the children to dig long trenches in the sand with spades and scoops. Provide a jug of water that the children can use to pour water into the trench.

Talk about the way that Elijah dug a trench around the altar to fill with water.

Puzzles, toys, games

Gather a selection of games and jigsaw puzzles with fire engines or fire fighters as their theme.

Snack time

Story time

As you prepare to tell the story today, divide the children and carers into two teams, with a clear division between them. You will need a leader for each group, one to play the part of Elijah and the other to be King Ahab. You will also need a number of large stones or stuffed plastic bags, some sticks, a small paddling pool where you can build Elijah's altar, and a watering can filled with water. You could use appropriately coloured ribbons to represent the fire, or just leave it to the imagination. Settle everyone down and begin the story.

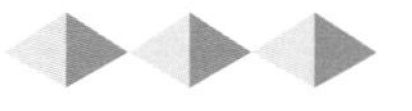

In today's story, we meet a very bad king—King Ahab *(encourage everyone to boo as Ahab poses in front of them)*. King Ahab didn't believe in God and he didn't look after God's people very well. He had a made-up God, called Baal, but Baal wasn't real and didn't do anything.

There had been no rain for a very long time and Elijah, a good man who followed God, tried to warn King Ahab that he needed to trust God to look after the people. But Ahab would not listen, so Elijah told him that they needed to have a contest to see which God was real—Baal or Elijah's God.

Elijah and Ahab each built an altar out of stone. *(The volunteers playing the parts of Elijah and Ahab should choose some helpers from their teams to help them as they act out the story.)* Then they piled some wood on top. Elijah told Ahab that they should put some meat on top of each of the altars, then, instead of lighting the wood, each of them should pray to their own God. So Ahab and his helpers danced around their altar and asked Baal to send the fire *(encourage the volunteers to join in)*—but nothing happened. There was no fire.

Then Elijah did something that surprised everyone: he poured water all over the altar he had made, which would make it much harder to catch fire. Elijah didn't make a big fuss like Ahab had. He just prayed quietly to God to send fire, to show the people that he was the real God.

At that very moment, Elijah's altar caught fire and burnt all the wood. Then everyone knew that Elijah's God was the only real God. They all prayed to him to thank him for sending the fire.

Prayer

Thank you, God, that you are the real God and you always listen to our prayers. Amen

Songs

Songs today could include:

- Nothing's too big (Doug Horley)
- Have we made our God too small? (Doug Horley)

Take home

Encourage your families to spend some time in prayer together this week, thinking of words to say to tell God how great we think he is.

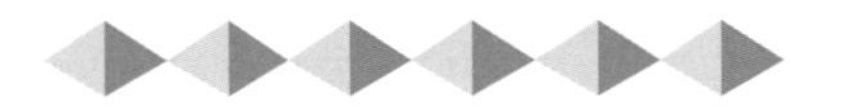

17

Daniel and the lions

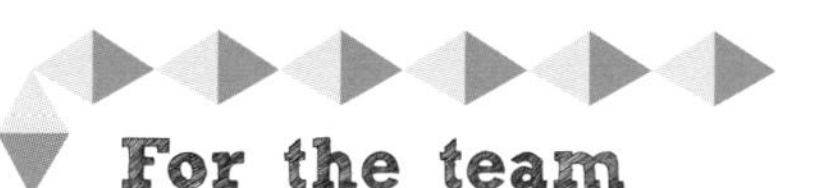

For the team

Refer to pages 6–8 to see how the activity areas work together

Session theme

Today we are reminded that following God sometimes puts us in difficult situations. Even when things look bleak, though, God still holds us safely in his hands.

Bible text: Daniel 6

Team prayer

Almighty God, help us to remember that you hold us safe in every circumstance. Help us to hold tightly to you and to remember our choice to follow you daily.

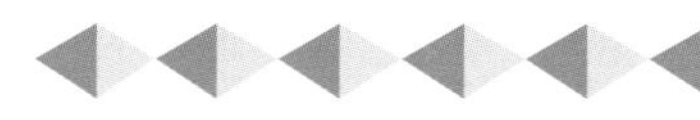

Activity areas

Sensory, tactile, malleable

Prepare some recordings of animal sounds (which can be sourced online). Invite the children and carers to listen to the different recordings, to try to identify the animals making each sound.

Talk about the sound that lions normally make, and how God silenced them so that they did not hurt Daniel.

Small world play

Create a zoo scene with appropriate animals, including lions, in different enclosures and people figures for zoo keepers and visitors. Help the children to take care of the animals, keeping them in the appropriate enclosures, safely away from the visitors.

Talk about the children's own experiences of visiting a zoo or safari park. Which animal is their favourite?

Role play / dressing up

Create a zoo area, with soft toy animals, 'enclosures' such as play pens or large cardboard boxes, bedding, food and water bowls, brooms, buckets and appropriate dressing-up outfits. Encourage children to take care of the animals, feeding them and cleaning out the enclosures.

Talk about the different jobs that zoo keepers do. Draw attention to the lions and talk about why they are so dangerous.

Creative

Provide paper plates, large lolly sticks or elastic, and yellow, orange and brown paint. Help the children to create a lion face mask by cutting out eye holes in the appropriate places before painting the lion's face, mane and facial features. Either stick the lolly stick on to the back of the mask so that children can hold it up to their face, or tie elastic through a hole on either side of the plate for children to wear the mask.

Talk about the different features of a lion as you paint. Talk about how scary it would be to be up close to a real lion.

Construction

Provide a selection of building blocks and work with the children and carers to build a den, perhaps including a doorway, windows through which you can check on the lions, a tunnel into the den or simply a hole to be dropped into.

Talk about what a scary place a lions' den would have been. Nobody would have wanted to be put in with the lions.

Books

Provide a selection of books about lions and other zoo or safari animals, along with story books about Daniel's life and a number of children's Bibles.

Invite the children to share the books with you, reading to them as they wish and talking about the things that the children find of interest.

Sand

Before the session, create some lion pawprint shapes by sticking corrugated card shapes on to a flat base. Invite the children to use them to make pawprint trails in wet sand before walking through the sand themselves.

Talk about how our footprints are different from those left by lions.

Puzzles, toys, games

Toys offered today should have a lion theme, and could include a selection of hand or finger puppets, along with lion-shaped jigsaw puzzles and games.

Snack time

Story time

For today's story, you will need a volunteer to play the part of Daniel, another to play the part of King Darius, and several children with lion masks to play the lions in the den. Prompt the children to move around at the appropriate points, perhaps miming any appropriate actions.

There was once a man called Daniel who always tried to do the things that made God happy, even when it was hard. Daniel and his friends were far from home, in a strange country with strange rules and beliefs. The king of this country, King Darius, liked Daniel because he was a good worker, but Darius didn't understand about God.

Some of the king's helpers, who didn't like Daniel, tricked the king into making a new rule that people should pray to him and not to any other god. If people prayed to anyone else, they would be thrown into the lions' den to be gobbled up by the fierce lions.

Encourage the children who are playing the part of the lions to make appropriate sound effects.

Daniel knew that he couldn't follow this new rule because he had to do the right thing and worship God, so he carried on praying to God. The king's helpers made sure that King Darius knew about it, and Daniel was caught praying to God.

So Daniel was thrown into the den of lions, ready to be gobbled up *(encourage more roaring)*. King Darius felt sad about this, but he had to follow the new rule too. He spent all night worrying about Daniel.

The next morning, King Darius went back to the lions' den to check on Daniel. He was amazed to find that Daniel had not been gobbled up by the lions. He was alive, safe and well. When King Darius asked Daniel what had happened, Daniel explained that God had sent an angel to keep him safe.

King Darius was so happy! He tore up the rule and told the people that they should all pray to God, because he now knew that God was real.

Prayer

Thank you, God, that we can pray to you without worrying, because there are no rules to stop us. Please help us to do the right thing, just as Daniel did. Amen

Songs

Songs today could include:

- I once was frightened of spiders (Ian Smale)
- My God is so big, so strong and so mighty (Anon)

Take home

You could suggest that your families take a visit to a zoo or safari park this week to see some lions for themselves, or watch some footage of them online. Encourage them to remember how God kept Daniel safe when he was facing the lions.

18

Jonah: God's messenger

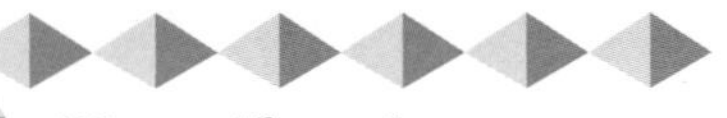

For the team

Refer to pages 6–8 to see how the activity areas work together

Session theme

During this session, we explore the story of Jonah, God's reluctant messenger, celebrating the God of second chances and reminding our families that God wants to involve us in his plans.

Bible text: Jonah 1—4

Team prayer

Dear God, thank you that you choose us to be involved in your plans. Help us to stand right where you call us to be.

Activity areas

Sensory, tactile, malleable

Create some 'slime' from cornflour, water and food colouring, and add some small plastic fish to it, in a container. Encourage children to scoop up handfuls of the mixture and feel through the slime to find the fish.

Talk about how Jonah would have felt in the slimy belly of the fish. What things would he have found in there with him?

Small world play

Provide a roadmap floor mat, with a few small cars. Encourage the children to act out what it means to go on a journey, choosing which way to turn at each junction.

Talk about Jonah and the choice he had to make, to go the way that God wanted, or go his own way.

Role play / dressing up

Before the session begins, construct a dome-shaped tent, leaving the entry flap open to form the mouth of a fish. Drape a large piece of blue fabric over the top, and stick on two eyes cut from paper. Inside the tent, place some plastic fish, sea creatures and crêpe paper seaweed, which the fish may have swallowed. Invite children to 'swim' into the belly of the fish.

Talk about what it would have been like for Jonah, stuck inside the fish for three days and nights.

Creative

Gather a selection of plastic containers, such as margarine tubs and yogurt pots, along with plastic drinking straws, gaffer tape, paper sail shapes, felt-tip pens, stickers and a hole punch. Help the children and carers to construct and decorate their own model boat. Punch a hole in the top and bottom of the sail before threading the straw through, and use the tape to attach the straw to the plastic container.

Talk about how Jonah took a boat ride in the opposite direction from the place God wanted him to go.

Construction

Gather some large cardboard boxes and help the children and carers to construct a large cardboard boat, which they can all sit inside. Encourage them to include a sail, wheel, anchor, seats and oars.

Talk about how Jonah was trying to escape from God, but found that God is always with us and there is nowhere we can go to escape from him.

Books

Provide a selection of non-fiction books about whales, fish and boats for the children to look at, along with a selection of children's Bibles and books retelling the story of Jonah.

Offer to read the books to the children, if they so wish, and talk about the things that they notice or find interesting.

Water

Provide a large toy sailing ship to float on top of the water and a large plastic fish, along with a selection of people figurines. Help the children to re-enact parts of the story, including Jonah's attempt to run away, the storm that occurred on the sea, and the moment when Jonah was swallowed by the large fish. Encourage the children to make large waves in the water.

Talk about how Jonah must have been feeling at each point in the story.

Sand

Invite the children to create a beach scene by shaping the sand into a slope and filing the shallow end with water to represent the sea. They can also build sandcastles and insert small model palm trees at the highest point on the slope.

Talk about how the fish spat Jonah out on to a beach. How relieved must Jonah have been when his days in the fish were finally over?

Puzzles, toys, games

You could provide a selection of jigsaw puzzles or games that feature boats and fish, as well as 'post office' or letter-themed toys or games to reinforce the concept of Jonah passing on a message from God.

Snack time

Story time

Today's story retelling has a repetitive chorus, which children can join in with as you tell the story. Kneel down on the floor in front of the children and display a small person figurine to represent Jonah, a toy boat and a large toy fish, which you can move around at the appropriate points in the script.

This man is called Jonah; he was one of God's helpers. God gave messages to Jonah to share with his people. One day, God told Jonah to go to a town called Nineveh, where the people were being mean. He wanted Jonah to tell them that they needed to change their ways.

God said 'Go,' but Jonah said 'No!'

So Jonah went to find a boat.

Jonah asked the sailors to take him with them on their boat, which was travelling in the opposite direction from the way that God wanted him to go. Jonah was trying to run away from God. The boat set sail but, while they were travelling, a terrible storm began to rage. The sailors were very scared.

God said 'Go,' but Jonah said 'No!'

So then God had to send a storm.

Jonah knew that the reason for the storm was that God was trying to stop him from running away. He told the sailors that, to stop the storm, they should throw him out of the boat and into the sea. The sailors didn't want to do this, but Jonah convinced them that it was the right thing to do.

God said 'Go,' but Jonah said 'No!'

Then out of the boat Jonah did go.

Jonah slipped down, down, down, deep into the water, where he was swallowed by an enormous fish. Jonah did not die in the water, but he was rescued and found himself sitting in the fish's tummy.

God said 'Go,' but Jonah said 'No!'

And into a fish Jonah did go.

While he was there, Jonah thought hard about the choice he had made to run away from God, and then he prayed. He said 'sorry' for not following God's instructions and promised that, if he got out of the fish, he would do what God told him to do.

God said 'Go,' but Jonah said 'No!'

And then he asked for another go.

So God made the fish take Jonah to a sandy beach, where it spat him out on the sand. God gave Jonah another chance, and this time Jonah did the right thing. He went to Nineveh and gave the people there God's message.

God said 'Go,' and Jonah said 'Yes!'

And Jonah did just what God had said.

God reminded Jonah that he loved the people of Nineveh, just as he loved Jonah, and would give them a second chance, just as he had given Jonah a second chance.

So when God says 'Go,' remember Jonah and say 'Yes!'

Prayer

Dear God, thank you that you love us, just as you loved Jonah and the people of Nineveh. Thank you that when we say 'sorry', you give us a second chance too. Amen

Songs

Songs today could include:

- I can do all things (Jim Bailey)
- If I've been wrong (Sammy Horner)

Take home

Encourage your families to talk about the opportunities that they have to share God's message of love and second chances with the people they meet this week.

New Testament stories

19

Mary and the angel

For the team

Refer to pages 6–8 to see how the activity areas work together

Session theme

In this first session from the New Testament, the story of Jesus' promised birth is explored as, together with the children, we anticipate the events of Christmas and the nativity story.

Bible text: Luke 1:26–38

Team prayer

Lord Jesus, as we wait to celebrate your birth, may we share the wonder and celebration of this story with those we meet today.

Activity areas

Sensory, tactile, malleable

Provide a few safe light sources, such as children's torches, for the children to explore, along with pieces of coloured cellophane and different fabrics through which to shine the light.

Talk about how angels in the Bible are often associated with a bright shining light.

Small world play

Set out a dolls' house, along with one woman figure and another figure to represent the angel, to help the children explore today's story.

Talk about how Mary was just getting on with her daily life when the angel appeared.

Role play / dressing up

Bring out the nativity costumes, particularly those used for Mary and the angels. You will not need a baby Jesus doll for this activity. Draw attention to the roles of Mary and Gabriel at this stage of the story.

Talk about how the other characters had no idea that they would also be involved in the story. Christmas is a great time for surprises, and these were the first surprises in the story.

Creative

Using the angel template on page 126, draw around the shape on to a paper plate and cut it out. Turn the sides of the shape around to meet at the back, fixing them together with a staple. Provide paints, pens, glitter glue and sparkles and invite children and carers to decorate their angel.

We don't know what angels really look like, because the Bible doesn't tell us very much about their appearance. Talk about this together. What do the children think angels might look like? How do they think Mary would have felt when the angel appeared in front of her?

Construction

This session offers an opportunity for further woodworking activities. Invite the children to help you by working safely to hammer nails into the wood and sand down the edges with sandpaper. Softwood or corkboard both offer safe alternatives for young children, who can use the appropriate tools under close supervision.

Talk about Joseph, the man who Mary was going to marry: he was a carpenter whose job it was to make things out of wood.

Books

Provide a selection of children's Bibles and nativity story books. You could also offer some non-fiction books about babies.

Share the books with the children and draw particular attention to the first part of the nativity story, where Mary is visited by an angel.

Water

Before the session, write a few short messages appropriate to the children, perhaps with illustrations, and place them into sealed small plastic bottles. Provide some small fishing nets so that the children can fish for the messages in the water. Open the bottles and read the messages to the children.

Talk about how an angel came to deliver an important message to Mary.

Puzzles, toys, games

You could offer children a selection of toys and puzzles related to the nativity story as you begin to prepare to celebrate this special time of year.

Snack time

Story time

For today's story retelling, you will need one of your helpers to play the part of Mary and another to be the angel. It would work well, if you are able, to use an arm-rod puppet as the angel, perhaps dressed in white, with a child-sized set of angel wings. The puppeteer will need to stand behind a screen, such as a puppet theatre screen or a door.

Mary should be miming, perhaps cleaning the house, as you begin the story.

There was once a young woman called Mary. She was going to get married soon, to a man called Joseph. One day, when she was getting on with her normal activities, an angel, one of God's special messengers, suddenly appeared in front of her.

'Don't be afraid,' said the angel, who could see that Mary was very shocked. 'God is pleased with you. He has chosen you to have a baby—a very special baby. This baby is God's own Son. You will call him Jesus.'

Afterwards, Mary thought about all the things that the angel had said. It was a big surprise, but Mary felt very special to know that God had chosen her to have baby Jesus.

Over the next few months, Mary got ready to have her very special son. She told Joseph, and, even though he was a bit scared too, Joseph promised God that he would look after Mary and baby

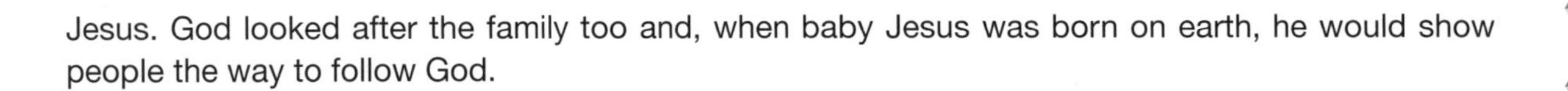

Jesus. God looked after the family too and, when baby Jesus was born on earth, he would show people the way to follow God.

Prayer

Dear God, thank you that you chose Mary to do a special job for you when she gave birth to baby Jesus. Thank you that Jesus is your special gift for the whole world. Amen

Songs

Songs today could include:

- Mary's angel (Niki Davies)
- Mary's song (Richard Hubbard)

Take home

Encourage your families to spend some time, as they prepare for Christmas, remembering today's story and thinking about how they can get ready to celebrate the birth of Jesus.

20

Jesus is born

For the team

Refer to pages 6–8 to see how the activity areas work together

Session theme

Today's session celebrates one of the best-known and most central stories of our faith. The children and their families may be familiar with some elements, but this session provides an opportunity to explore the story afresh.

Bible text: Luke 2:1–20

Team prayer

Lord Jesus, today we celebrate your birth. Help us to keep your story central to our session today and to our daily lives.

Activity areas

Sensory, tactile, malleable

Prepare a supply of salt dough and provide some nativity-themed cookie cutters and glitter. Invite the children and carers to create their own Christmas tree decorations. You could use a straw to make a hole in the top of each shape so that they can be hung by a ribbon when they have hardened.

Talk about the different shapes that the children choose and why it is important that we include these figures among our Christmas decorations at home.

Small world play

Source a sturdy nativity set, with which the children can re-enact the story of the nativity. You may be able to find a hand or finger puppet set, which children can use as an alternative to wooden or plastic figurines.

Talk about the different stages of the story as the children re-enact each element, helping them to appreciate the wonder in the appearance of angels, the star to follow and the birth of God's Son in a smelly stable.

Role play / dressing up

Bring out the box of nativity costumes and invite children to dress up as their favourite characters in the story. You could set up a nativity scene, with a stable background and a manger, and invite carers to take photos of their children in the nativity scene.

Talk about the reasons why the children have chosen a particular character in the nativity story.

Creative

Gather a supply of shoeboxes, which children can use to create their own stable scene, perhaps with some hay to stick on the top of the box to create a roof. Provide some cardboard tubes and a selection of papers, fabrics and wool, with which children can create the main characters in the nativity story.

Talk about each of the characters as the children make them, and their role within the nativity story. Encourage the children to take their nativity scene home and re-enact the story with their families.

Construction

Work with the children and carers to create a model of a stable in which you can stand a larger set of nativity figurines. You could use a cardboard box as a base or set this up as a woodworking activity.

Talk about where the children were born, whether in a hospital or at home. Can they imagine what it would be like to be born in a stable?

Books

Gather a selection of children's Bibles and books about the nativity story for children to look at and share.

Offer to read the stories to the children, as they request it, and talk about the things they find of interest in the nativity story.

Sand

Provide a few small plastic camels, perhaps with figurines of the wise men, and stick a large shiny star at one end of the sandpit area. Encourage the children to walk the camels across the sand, looking at the tracks they leave as they walk.

Talk about why the wise men travelled for such a long way, for such a long time, following the star to find Jesus and knowing that he was a very special baby.

Puzzles, toys, games

A wide selection of nativity-themed toys, games and puzzles are available, which could be set out for children to access today. You could also set up a Christmas tree for the children to help to decorate, including nativity-themed decorations along with generic tinsel and baubles.

Snack time

Story time

For today's special Christmas-themed session, invite all the children to be involved in the retelling by dressing up in the nativity costumes and stepping into the scene at the appropriate point in the story. You could set it up as though you were going to perform a nativity play, with the carers as the audience.

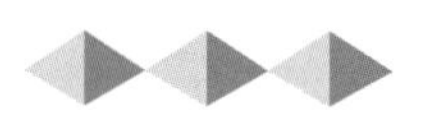

Last week we heard how Mary had been visited by an angel, a messenger from God. The angel told Mary that she was going to have a very special baby—Jesus, God's Son.

When it was nearly time for the baby to be born, Mary and Joseph had to go on a very long journey, all the way to Bethlehem, where Joseph's family were from. They went there so that they and everyone else could be counted by the Romans.

Mary and Joseph took a donkey and began their journey all the way to Bethlehem. When they got there, it was very busy, with people everywhere. There was nowhere for Mary and Joseph to stay because all the houses were full.

A kind innkeeper let Mary and Joseph stay in his stable with all the animals, so that they would have somewhere safe to rest. While they were there, the time came for Mary to have the baby. There was no cot, so Mary wrapped her precious baby in a blanket and laid him in the manger, where the animals ate their hay.

Outside on the hills, some shepherds were looking after the sheep when an angel appeared in the sky. The angel said, 'Go to Bethlehem, where you will find a very special baby. This baby is God's Son, Jesus.'

Then the sky was filled with hundreds of angels who were all singing a special song, praising God. The shepherds were very surprised by this, but they did as the angel told them and went to Bethlehem, where they found Mary, Joseph and baby Jesus in the stable.

A long, long way away, some wise men saw a special star appear in the sky. They knew that the star would lead them to a newborn king, so they followed it a long, long way—all the way to Bethlehem.

When they arrived in Bethlehem, they found Mary, Joseph and Jesus, and gave the baby special gifts of gold, frankincense and myrrh. Mary, Joseph and all the visitors knew that Jesus was a very special baby. He was God's Son who had come down to live on earth.

Prayer

Thank you, God, for this special Christmas story and for giving your Son, Jesus, to be born on earth. Help us to remember this story as we celebrate Christmas with our families and friends. Amen

Songs

Songs today could include:

- Away in a manger (Anon)
- The following adaptation of 'Twinkle, twinkle, little star':

Twinkle, twinkle, great big star,
Led the wise men from afar.
Special presents that they bring
To give to the baby king.
Twinkle, twinkle, great big star,
Led the wise men from afar.

Take home

Encourage your families to consider including a nativity scene in their Christmas decorations.

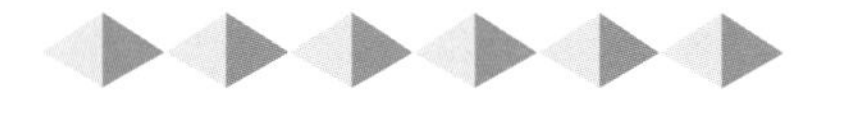

21

Jesus in the temple

For the team

Refer to pages 6–8 to see how the activity areas work together

Session theme

This session explores the only story we have about Jesus' childhood and shows how he was already marked out by his behaviour. Many children will be able to relate to the experience of being lost, but they will need help to discover the greater truth of this incident—Jesus' identity as the Son of God.

Bible text: Luke 2:41–52

Team prayer

Lord Jesus, as we try to follow your example, learning more and more about your kingdom, help us to share some of this enthusiasm with the children we meet today.

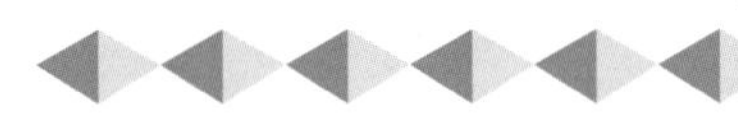

Activity areas

Sensory, tactile, malleable

Prepare some large trays filled with different tactile materials (such as jelly, sand, cooked pasta, feathers and shaving foam) and invite the children to walk through each of the trays. Provide a bowl of water and a towel so that children can wash their feet.

Talk about the different textures that they encountered as they walked through each of the trays. Explain that in today's story Jesus and his family had to walk a very long way. How do we think their feet would have felt at the end of their journey?

Role play / dressing up

Provide a selection of ride-on vehicles and hobby horses and encourage children to re-enact going on a journey.

Talk about the different journeys that the children have taken with their families. Explain that in today's story we will find out what happened to Jesus when he went on a journey with his parents, a long time before cars were invented.

Creative

Prepare some tea- or coffee-stained paper before the session. Invite the children and carers to design their own maps on the paper, using felt-tip pens.

Talk about using a map to find our way on a long journey and how it may have been helpful for Mary and Joseph to have a map to follow.

Construction

Provide a selection of building blocks and invite children and carers to construct a model of the temple. You could provide some illustrations for guidance, but allow them to pursue their own creative ideas rather than insisting upon technical accuracy.

Talk about the temple, which was a special place for Jewish people like Jesus. It was a place where people could learn about God.

Books

As well as offering children's Bibles and story books today, try to include books with pictures of the temple as it would have been at the time of Jesus, and story books about children who are lost and found again.

Share the books with the children as they wish, reading the stories, sharing the illustrations and talking about the things that the children find interesting.

Water

Set up a marble maze in the water tray (a 3D version, with towers and ramps that marbles usually roll around). Provide a small water jug, which can be used by the children to pour water into the top, to explore how the water travels.

Talk about Mary and Joseph searching in every direction to try to find Jesus, a bit like searching in a maze.

Sand

Invite the children to take off their shoes and socks so that they can walk through the sand, leaving a trail of footprints behind them.

Talk about how Mary and Joseph retraced their steps, going back to Jerusalem to find Jesus.

Puzzles, toys, games

Toys and puzzles offered today could include mazes and copies of pictures where children have to look for something hidden.

Snack time

Story time

This story can be told using small people figurines to represent Mary, Joseph, Jesus and the priests. You will also need a cardboard box to represent the temple, which could be decorated accordingly. Before you begin, place the priests and Jesus under the box on the floor in front of you, and invite the children to sit around where they can see.

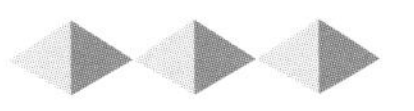

In our last session, we heard how Jesus was born in a stable in Bethlehem. Most of the other stories we know about Jesus happened when he was grown up, but we do know one about Jesus as a child, when he was about twelve years old.

Mary and Joseph *(hold up the figurines)* had taken Jesus to Jerusalem for a special party, the Passover feast. They had travelled for many days, a long way from home. Mary, Joseph and Jesus all enjoyed the special celebrations and, when the party was over, Mary and Joseph started the long walk back home *(move Mary and Joseph around the scene, away from the temple)*. Jesus wasn't with them, but they thought he must be walking with his friends, as there were so many people in the crowds. When they stopped to rest for the night, they realised that Jesus was missing. They had lost their son! He must have been left in Jerusalem.

Mary and Joseph started walking all the way back to Jerusalem to find Jesus. They searched high and low—in the shops and in the houses, in the fields and in the busy streets. They searched for three whole days, looking for him. They were very worried.

Then they went to the temple, and that's just where Jesus was. Look! *(Lift the cardboard temple away to show Jesus sitting with the priests.)* Jesus had spent all his time in the temple, asking the priests some very tricky questions about God, listening to everything that they could tell him.

Mary and Joseph were so glad to have Jesus back, safe and sound. They knew he was a very special boy.

Prayer

Dear God, thank you for our mummies and daddies who look after us and keep us safe, and thank you that you give us people who can teach us more about you. Amen

Songs

Songs today could include:

- Father, we adore you (Terry Coelho)

Take home

Invite your families to come and visit your church building at some point in the week, to talk about what makes it a special place to be in.

22 Jesus' baptism

For the team

Refer to pages 6–8 to see how the activity areas work together

Session theme

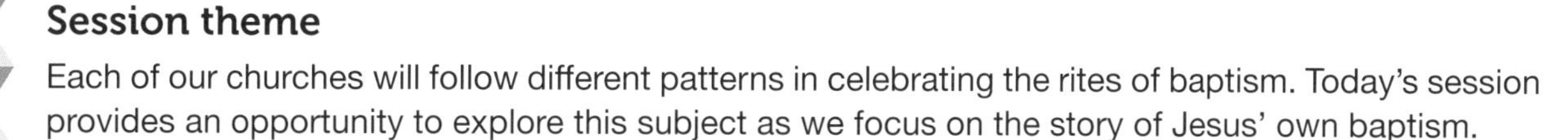

Each of our churches will follow different patterns in celebrating the rites of baptism. Today's session provides an opportunity to explore this subject as we focus on the story of Jesus' own baptism.

Bible text: Matthew 3:13–17

Team prayer

Almighty God, in today's story we meet you as Father, Son and Holy Spirit in one. Help us never to belittle your greatness but to celebrate your great story.

Activity areas

Sensory, tactile, malleable

Before the session, copy the play dough mat template for Jesus' baptism scene (page 128) and laminate it. Provide some blue play dough for the children to use to add water to the scene.

Talk about the different things that the children can see in the scene and how they relate to the story.

Role play / dressing up

Provide a selection of water-related dressing-up items, including things used for swimming, fishing, diving and sailing.

Talk about the way that we use water for different activities, pointing out that baptism is a very special use of water.

Creative

Prepare some simple dove shapes cut out of white card, using the template on page 126. Invite the children and carers to decorate their own dove by sticking white feathers all over the bird shape. To hang, tie a small length of cotton to the top of the dove's head.

Talk about the dove that appeared in the sky above Jesus when he was baptised, as a sign of the Holy Spirit descending.

Construction

Provide a selection of sticks and leaves for the children to use to build a shelter for John the Baptist.

Talk about John the Baptist and how he chose to live on his own in the wilderness, rather than living in a town among other people.

Books

Books offered today could include books about baptism and rivers, alongside children's Bibles and other books that retell the story of Jesus' baptism.

Read to the children as they wish, sharing the stories and pictures to discover what the children find interesting.

Water

Create a 'river' using a length of drainpipe or other tube, cut in half and filled with water, with a few plastic play figurines standing in it.

Talk about the way that John the Baptist baptised people, including Jesus, in the river—not in a font or baptistry pool, as the children might have seen.

Sand

Gather a selection of objects related to baptism, as expressed in your own church tradition, such as a shell, a candle, a pot of oil, a water container, a small towel and so on. Bury them in the sand for the children to uncover.

Talk about how each of the objects is used in the celebration of baptism.

Puzzles, toys, games

Your church may have a collection of props or toys that are used to help children understand baptism. This session would be a great opportunity to share these toys with the children.

Snack time

Story time

The children will perform some simple hand actions as you tell today's story. Whenever you use the word 'river', you should all stretch your hands out in front of you and move them across from one side to the other while wriggling your fingers to represent the movement of water. When you talk about the dove, all link your thumbs and wave your fingers, like a bird flying. You will also use the words 'down' and 'up'; encourage the children to point in the right direction when you do so.

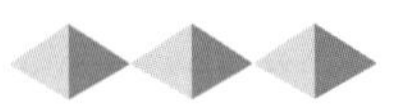

There once was a man called John. He was Jesus' cousin and he lived in the desert. He wore very funny clothes and ate insects for his dinner. John listened to the things that God told him and he helped people to get ready for the time when Jesus would come. John told people that they had to listen to Jesus. He would stand in the **river** and baptise people who wanted to show that they were God's followers.

One day, Jesus came to the **river** to see John. John was very surprised when Jesus asked to be baptised, but he knew that Jesus was a very special man and he wanted to do what Jesus said. Jesus walked into the **river**, and John lowered him **down** into the water and back **up** again to baptise him.

Just then, **up** in the sky, a **dove** appeared and God's voice spoke, saying, 'This is my son, who I love. I am very happy with him.'

Then Jesus walked back out of the **river**. He was ready to do the special work that God would give him.

Prayer

Dear God, thank you for your Son, Jesus, who came to earth to do your special work. Amen

Songs

Songs today could include:

- Father, we adore you (Terry Coelho)

Take home

Encourage your families to share their own baptism stories at home this week, perhaps looking at family videos or photo albums.

23

Jesus chooses his disciples

For the team

Refer to pages 6–8 to see how the activity areas work together

Session theme

This session celebrates Jesus' invitation to his disciples to come and follow him. This invitation is extended to us all, regardless of our age or background.

Bible text: Matthew 4:18–22

Team prayer

Lord Jesus, thank you for the invitation to follow you. Help us as we take this journey day by day, and remind us to invite others to join us as we travel.

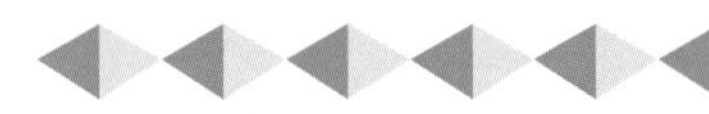

Activity areas

Sensory, tactile, malleable

Freeze water, coloured with food colouring, in a fish-shaped ice tray and then move the ice fish into a shallow tray of water. Encourage the children and carers to try to catch the fish in their hands.

Talk about how difficult it is to catch the fish, because they are so slippery.

Small world play

Lay out a piece of blue fabric and a piece of green fabric to represent the lake and the land. Provide some toy boats and people figurines for the children to use to re-enact the story.

Talk about how the fishermen gave up their life on the water to follow Jesus.

Role play / dressing up

Create a fishing scene, perhaps with a boat (such as an inflatable dinghy), wellington boots and raincoats to wear, and simple fishing rods (lengths of string tied on to sticks) or nets (a piece of net curtain could be used).

Talk about children's own experiences of going for a boat ride or going fishing, and how they can re-enact those events in the boat scene.

Creative

Cut some fish shapes out of coloured card. Provide poster paints in a variety of colours and bottle tops in a range of sizes. Invite the children to use the bottle tops to print overlapping circles on to the fish, to look like scales. Alternatively, you could provide shiny paper, cut into oval-shaped scales, for children to glue on to the fish. Show some photos of fish as a stimulus for the children's designs.

Talk about the many different types of fish that God has created.

Construction

Provide some large cardboard boxes and work with the children to create a cardboard boat in which they can all sit together. You could bring in a large broom handle and sheet to create a sail, or include smaller boxes as seats inside the boat.

Talk about children's own experiences of being on board a boat. Can they imagine what it would be like to work on a boat every day?

Books

Provide a selection of children's Bibles and story books about Jesus and his disciples, along with books about boats, fish and fishing.

Spend time sitting with the children and offer to read to any who would like to listen to the stories. Share the non-fiction books and talk about the children's own related experiences.

Water

Provide some plastic toy boats to float on the water in the tray, along with some small toy fish. Ask the children to see how many fish they can put into the boat while it floats, counting the fish carefully as they put them in.

Talk about the children's own experiences of going fishing or being on a boat. Have they ever caught a fish themselves? Have they ever seen fishermen catching fish in their nets?

Puzzles, toys, games

Toys for this session could include a magnetic fishing game, as well as other toys, games and puzzles relating to boats and fish.

Snack time

Story time

For today's story, you may be able to seat everyone in the cardboard boat that you created in the construction area. Alternatively, you could invite a few volunteers to sit in the boat. Provide a large piece of netting (perhaps a piece of net curtain) and show your families how to hold it over one side of the boat.

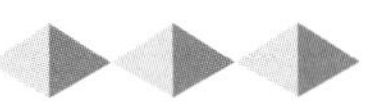

When Jesus began his work on earth, he chose some men to help him and to learn more about God from him. They were ordinary people who had ordinary jobs. Some of them worked on a boat, just like this one. This is the story of how Jesus invited those men to be his friends.

One day, when Jesus was teaching people about God, crowds gathered on the banks of a lake where some fishermen had been out working all night. Jesus got into a boat so that all the people could see him. When he had finished talking to the crowds, he told the fishermen to take the boat further out on the lake to catch some fish.

One of the fishermen said, 'We've been out all night, and we haven't caught a single fish! But, if you tell me to try again, I will.'

So the fishermen rowed their boat out into the middle of the lake *(encourage those sitting in the boat to pretend to row the boat)*. Then they put the nets down into the water *(prompt the volunteers to hold the net over the side of the boat).* Suddenly, the nets were full of fish—big fish, and little fish, hundreds and hundreds of them. There were so many fish in the nets that everybody had to help to bring them in *(encourage everyone to pretend to heave the nets in).*

The fishermen realised that Jesus was very, very special. He gave them a special invitation—to stop being fishermen and to spend time with him, learning more about God. They would 'catch' people who wanted to learn more about God too, instead of catching fish. It was the start of an amazing adventure.

Prayer

Dear Jesus, thank you that we can follow you, just like these fishermen did, and learn more about you. Amen

Songs

Songs today could include:

- Come and join in the party (Paul Field)
- The following adaptation of 'Row, row, row your boat':

Row, row, row the boat out into the lake.
Catch so many fish that the nets begin to break.

Follow, follow, follow Jesus, every single day.
Learn about the things he said and live your life his way.

Invite everyone to find a partner to sit with. Then hold hands and row, as if you are in a boat, as you sing this song.

Take home

You could suggest that your families would like to take a boat trip or a fishing trip, if they are able. Alternatively, they could visit a lake to watch the boats sailing.

24

The wise and foolish builders

For the team

Refer to pages 6–8 to see how the activity areas work together

Session theme

This session is the first to explore a story that Jesus told. The story relates a situation that would have been familiar to the people of Jesus' time, as well as exploring a key principle of the Christian faith: what do we build our lives upon?

Bible text: Matthew 7:24–29

Team prayer

Lord Jesus, thank you that the stories you told are as relevant to us today as they were to the people you met face to face. Help us to explain this story to the children we meet today in ways that they can understand.

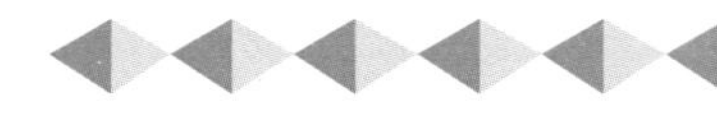

Activity areas

Sensory, tactile, malleable

Provide clay and tools and invite children and carers to create their own bricks before using them to build a wall. Children may like to see some real bricks, to look more closely at their shape and texture.

Talk about the way that bricks are made, being fired to make them hard and strong enough to use when building a house.

Small world play

Create a building site scene, where children can use diggers, dumper trucks and other suitable toy vehicles. They can move small pebbles or beads around or dig into a base of soil, sand or woodchip to create trenches and holes.

Talk about children's own experiences of watching these heavy vehicles at work on a building site, reminding them that we should only watch them from a safe distance.

Role play / dressing up

Provide a selection of child-sized hi-vis vests, gloves and toy hard hats, along with plastic tools, so that they can pretend to be workers on a construction site. This activity could be combined with the construction activity detailed below, if you wish.

Talk about the process that builders go through to build a house: they start by digging out the foundation trenches and putting in the foundations, before building up from the base. Why is this process so important?

Creative

Gather some cardboard boxes and some square and rectangular card shapes, along with PVA glue. Invite the children and carers to create their own house, sticking on the card shapes to represent the windows and doors. Children could then use felt-tip pens or stickers to add extra details, such as flowers around the door or birds on the roof.

Talk about the story today, in which two people built a house, but only one builder thought about how to build his house safely.

Construction

Provide a selection of building bricks, building blocks, Jenga blocks or similar objects in a range of sizes or scales, so that children can build their own model houses.

Talk about the houses that the children build, and the features they include in their buildings. What do they think would make their perfect building?

Books

Offer a selection of books about buildings and construction vehicles. Display them together with children's Bibles and picture books about today's story.

Offer to read any of the books to children who wish to listen, and talk about the specific vocabulary in the information books.

Water

Provide some watering cans so that children can imitate rain falling into the water tray. Other objects can be added to the water tray for children to pour the rain over.

Talk about what it feels like to be caught in heavy rain. How do the children feel when they can watch the rain outside, safely, from their house windows?

Sand

Divide the sand tray into two parts, with a thick layer of uneven dry sand in one part and a sturdy wooden tray in the other. Invite children to use small blocks to build a tower in each of the two sections.

Talk about the differences between the two towers. Which one seems to be the most secure? Which one seems most likely to topple over?

Puzzles, toys, games

You may be able to provide a selection of jigsaw puzzles and games with a house theme. You could also create a simple 'beetle-drive' game, with a blank house-shaped base board and a selection of doors and windows for the children to add to their boards when they roll the correct number on a dice.

Snack time

Story time

Invite two volunteers to help with the storytelling today (perhaps parents or two of your helpers). Ask everyone else to be seated in front of you, where they can see the volunteers working. Set out a number of wooden building blocks (those with smooth faces, which cannot be attached to

one another). Ask one volunteer to build in the sand tray, with heaped dry sand, and give the other volunteer an empty tray. Ask both of your volunteers to build a model house using the bricks you have given them, encouraging them to build a beautiful house, tall and wide and grand.

While they are doing so, tell the story.

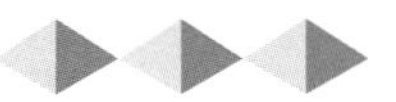

Jesus once told a story about house building. He talked about someone who built their house on the sand and someone who built their house on the rock *(point as appropriate)*. He said that people who are wise, who make good decisions, build their houses on the rock, and people who are foolish or silly build houses on the sand. Why do you think that might be?

What do you think might happen to this house on the sand when the rain comes? What about this house on the rock?

Bring out a watering can and pour water over each of the houses to demonstrate how unstable the sand is, and how safe the rock is.

Jesus said that he is like the rock. If we trust in him and the things he says, we will always be safe, even when problems come along, like the rain. The things we learn about Jesus from the stories we read in the Bible help us to learn to trust in God. They remind us that he will always keep us safe.

Prayer

Dear God, sometimes problems come along and make us feel unsettled. Thank you that we can always trust you to keep us safe. Amen

Songs

Songs today could include:

- Don't hide your light (Leanne Mitchell)
- The wise man built his house upon the rock (Ann Omley)

Take home

You could suggest that families keep looking out for new houses being built when they are out and about this week, as a reminder of today's story.

25

Jesus heals a paralysed man

For the team

Refer to pages 6–8 to see how the activity areas work together

Session theme

Today's session is the first that explores a miracle performed by Jesus. Through this story, we discover a God who has power to heal and a group of men who cared enough about their friend to introduce him to Jesus.

Bible text: Mark 2:1–17

Team prayer

Lord Jesus, today we remember your power to heal and we bring before you those who need to feel your healing touch today* (give names if appropriate)*. Help us to sensitively bring those we care about to meet with you today.

Activity areas

Sensory, tactile, malleable

You will need to prepare this activity a few days before the session to allow the mixture to fully harden. Mix together two cups of soil, two cups of flour, two cups of sand, one cup of salt and three-quarters of a cup of water and spread out the mixture in a flat container. Provide a selection of appropriate metal tools for children to use (under close supervision) to chisel holes into the dried-out mixture.

Talk about how the man's friends had to dig into the flat roof of the house to make a hole so that they could lower him down into the room where Jesus was speaking.

Small world play

Set up a street scene with different houses and other buildings and a selection of people figurines. Try to represent people of different ages and different abilities, ideally including some wheelchair users. You could re-enact part of the story by putting a lot of people in one of the houses, as though they have come to see Jesus.

Talk about how different these buildings are from the houses in the place where Jesus was, which had flat roofs. Talk about the different people, too. Jesus healed the man who couldn't walk. He loves all people the same—those who can walk and those who have to use a wheelchair to get about.

Creative

Provide some A5 pieces of coloured card and a selection of collage materials, glue, scissors and pens. Invite the children and carers to create a 'Get well card' for somebody they know who is poorly.

Talk about Jesus' power to heal people who are sick from all sorts of diseases, and how we can still pray to God today to ask him to make people better.

Construction

Use a square cardboard box to represent the house in the story, using felt-tip pens to draw a doorway, windows, a staircase up to the roof and a hole in the roof. Alternatively, help the children to use scissors to cut holes carefully in the appropriate places.

Talk about how the man's friends had to work together to carry him up on to the roof, because there were so many people in the house, listening to Jesus, that they couldn't get in through the door.

Books

Provide a selection of children's Bibles and retellings of this story, along with books about different types of houses and buildings and stories about friendship.

Share the books with the children, reading the stories to them as they wish and talking about the things that they notice.

Water

Source some wind-up water toys, such as swimmers or paddling ducks, which children can wind up and release to swim in the water.

Talk about how it feels to go swimming and what the children enjoy about being able to play and move about in the water. The man in this story would have been able to go swimming for the first time in many years, after Jesus had made him better.

Sand

Provide a selection of spades and invite the children to dig holes in the sand with the spades and their own hands.

Talk about how the man's friends had to dig a hole in the roof of the house where Jesus was speaking.

Puzzles, toys, games

The toys and games offered today could support the theme of friendship and caring. You could also provide toys about people who help us, such as nurses and doctors.

Snack time

Story time

Invite the children and carers to come and sit down in a circle with you. Explain that today you need them to help with the storytelling by performing a few simple actions. Ask everyone to hold both their hands out flat in front of them, palms facing upwards. During the story, you will need them to lift their hands—up, up, up—and lower them—down, down, down—at the appropriate points.

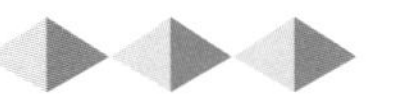

This is another story about something that happened when Jesus was on earth. There was once a man who could not walk and spent all his time lying on a bed. His friends knew that if they took him to see Jesus, he would make the man better, so that he could walk again.

So the man's friends carefully lifted him and his bed up, up, up! And off they went to see Jesus. When they got to the house where Jesus was, there were so many people that they couldn't get in through the door. But this house had a flat roof, so the men carried their friend up, up, up on to the roof.

Then they had to dig a hole in the roof so that they could get their friend near to Jesus. When the hole was big enough, they lowered their friend down, down, down into the room, right in front of Jesus.

Jesus saw the man and knew what he had to do for him. 'Firstly,' said Jesus, 'every bad thing you've ever done is forgiven; and secondly, get up! You are better—you can walk again.'

So the man stood up, up, up, picked up his bed and walked home on his own two legs. Jesus had made his whole life better again.

Prayer

Thank you, Jesus, that you have power to forgive us when we do things wrong, and to make us better, just like you did for the man in today's story. Amen

Songs

Songs today could include:

- Hands, hands, fingers, thumbs (Doug Horley)
- The wiggle song (Christy Weygandt and Dan Leuders)

Take home

Encourage your families to think about the people they know who are unwell. Perhaps they could visit some of those people this week to remind them that they care.

26

The farmer and his seeds

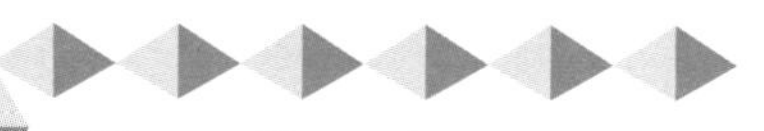

For the team

Refer to pages 6–8 to see how the activity areas work together

Session theme

This session explores another of Jesus' parables, which will resonate with children who like to watch things grow. As you meet the children and their families each week, you too sow seeds into their lives.

Bible text: Mark 4:1–9, 13–20

Team prayer

Lord Jesus, as we sow seeds into the lives of these families, would you prepare good soil, and tend and care for the tiny shoots of faith that grow throughout their lives.

Activity areas

Sensory, tactile, malleable

Set up a number of feely bags or boxes with props relating to the different 'textures' found in the story. They could include a bag of seeds, soil, pebbles and a tangle of wool or string to represent the weeds. Invite the children to feel inside the bags before looking at each of the props.

Talk about what children notice about the props as they feel them, and talk about how each of these things relates to the story.

Small world play

Set up a farm scene, with farm vehicles such as tractors, trailers and combine harvesters for the children to use to 'work the land'.

Talk about the way that farmers work nowadays, both when they sow the seeds and when they harvest their crops, and explain how this is different from the way that farmers would have worked in Jesus' time.

Role play / dressing up

Gather a selection of plant pots and seed trays, compost, seeds, watering cans and trowels. Invite the children and carers not only to role-play being a gardener or farmer, but actually to plant and care for some seeds, in order to see them grow at home.

Talk about the things we have to do to care for plants. Help the children to understand that we only do a small part of the job: God makes the plants grow by providing sunlight, rainwater and helpful nutrients in the soil.

Creative

Provide a selection of bird templates (see page 127) copied on to coloured card in a variety of colours, along with a selection of coloured craft feathers, fine elastic, small canes, googly eyes and PVA glue. Invite children and carers to use the feathers and eyes to decorate their own bird shape, before punching a hole in the top of the bird and using the fine elastic to attach the bird to the cane. The children can then move the cane up and down to make the bird 'jump' as though pecking at the seed.

Talk about how, in the story, the birds flew down and ate all the seed that was scattered on the path.

Books

Provide a selection of children's Bibles and story books that retell this parable, along with other books about farming and gardening. Share the books with the children, reading to them as they wish and talking about the things that they notice.

Water

Provide watering cans for children to use as they play in the water tray, and a selection of straws for children to use to suck water up from a cup.

Talk about how plants need water to help them to grow, and the way that they 'suck' water from the soil around them, up through their stems.

Sand

Provide a selection of small rocks, seeds and gravel. Add them to the damp sand so that the children can explore the different objects that they hear about during the story time.

Talk about the things that the children notice about each of the added props, and how they would make it difficult for the seeds to grow.

Puzzles, toys, games

Among the toys and games offered today, you could include jigsaw puzzles with the different parts of a plant to be put together, and bird-related toys.

Snack time

Story time

Invite the children to sit in four separate groups and tell them that they will all have a part to play in today's storytelling. Explain that you are going to tell a story about a farmer who planted some seeds and that you will show each group the action they need to perform when it comes to their part in the story.

This is a story that Jesus told to help people understand an important lesson. Once there was a farmer who went out to plant a great big bag of seeds. Some of the seeds fell on the road, where there was no soil for the seeds to be planted and grow. Some birds flew down and pecked up all the seeds.

Prompt the first group to bend down, hold their arms out as wings and pretend to peck all the seeds from the ground in front of them.

'Some of the seeds fell on the rocky soil. They grew up straight and tall, very quickly.
Invite the second group to stand on their tiptoes with their arms stretched high above their heads.

But they didn't grow any roots. So, when the sun came out, these plants just shrivelled up and died.
Encourage the group to sink back down to the ground.

The next lot of seeds fell into a weedy patch. The plants tried to grow but they were choked by the weeds and thorns that grew there.
Show the third group how to grow slowly, staying very low to the ground, twisted by the imaginary weeds.

But the last of the seeds that the farmer threw fell on to good soil, where they grew strong roots down into the soil, before growing up nice and tall, full of grains that the farmer could harvest.
The final group should be encouraged to grow steadily and stand up strongly.

Jesus told everyone who heard his story that if we are like that good soil, and we listen to the things that we hear about God, then we too can grow well and become more like him.

Prayer

Dear God, thank you for the stories about Jesus that we can read in the Bible and for the lessons that we can learn about you. Help us to be like good soil, ready to listen to you. Amen

Songs

Songs today could include:

- Growing, growing (John Hardwick)
- Sow'n'sow (Ian Smale)

Take home

Invite your families to take home a plant pot or seed tray which has had a seed planted into it in the role play area. Encourage them, as they see it sprout up at home, to think about how we can grow to be more like Jesus.

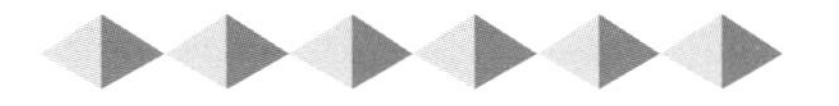

27

Jesus feeds 5000 people

For the team

Refer to pages 6–8 to see how the activity areas work together

Session theme

In today's session we remember another of Jesus' miracles and the willingness of a young boy to bring what he had to give to Jesus. This reminds us that Jesus can multiply the tiny gifts that we bring to him.

Bible text: Mark 6:30–44

Team prayer

Lord Jesus, as we bring our tiny gifts of service to you each week, would you please multiply them for your kingdom.

Activity areas

Sensory, tactile, malleable

Source an easy bread recipe and invite children and carers to participate in all stages of the process. If you do not have time to follow a full recipe, you could use a recipe for bread without yeast, or create salt dough so that children can pretend to be baking, reminding them that this dough cannot be consumed.

Talk about each of the stages of the process as you follow the recipe, encouraging the children to handle the dough and talk about how it feels.

Small world play

Set up an appropriate scene, such as a café, restaurant or food shop, where children can use people figurines to re-enact buying and enjoying a meal together.

Talk about all the different places that we can go, to find food to eat. In today's story, there were lots and lots of people who hadn't expected to be out at meal time and had nothing with them to eat. There was no supermarket or café, but Jesus still gave them more than enough.

Role play / dressing up

Set up a picnic scene, with a blanket spread out on the floor and a picnic basket with plates, cups and pretend food (or clean, empty food packaging). Encourage the children to pretend to have a picnic together, taking items out of the basket and sharing them.

Talk about children's own experiences of having a picnic with their family or friends. What sorts of things did they take with them on their picnic?

Creative

Provide some small bread rolls and tinned tuna or fish paste and invite the children to make their own fish sandwich, which could be eaten during snack time or wrapped up for the children to take home. Check for any food allergies.

Talk about the different ways that we can buy fish—in tins or jars, as fish fingers or battered fish, or fresh, as the people would have done in Jesus' time.

Books

Provide an appropriate selection of children's Bibles and retellings of this story, perhaps with books about the other miracles that Jesus performed. You can also include story books about going on a picnic.

Share the stories with the children, offering to read to any who would like to listen, and talk about the things that they find interesting.

Water

Place some plastic fish into the water tray and provide small fishing nets, which the children can use to scoop the fish out of the water. Encourage the children to count the fish as they catch them.

Talk about the fish that the boy shared in today's story. Even though he only had two small fish, Jesus used them to feed 5000 people.

Sand

Prepare wet sand in the tray and provide spoons, plates, old saucepans and so on, for the children to use to make their own mud pie bread rolls.

Talk about the way that Jesus multiplied the few bread rolls that he had available.

Puzzles, toys, games

Toys offered for children to play with today could include a magnetic fishing game as well as other puzzles, toys and games about fish and picnics.

Snack time

Story time

As you prepare to tell the story, invite your families to sit down together in small family groups. You will need some volunteers to play the part of the disciples. Each disciple will need a basket to hold, which they can use to take imaginary food out to the crowds of people.

This is another story about something that happened when Jesus was on earth. Lots and lots of people wanted to hear the things that Jesus said. They loved listening to his stories and learning more about God. One day, more than 5000 people came to listen to Jesus; that's a lot more people than we have here today. The people had been listening to Jesus all day long. His stories were so interesting that they didn't want to leave.

Jesus was getting worried about the people. He knew they would be hungry, but there were no shops nearby where they could buy their food. His disciples thought he should send the people home so that they could get some dinner, but the people didn't want to go. So Jesus decided to give them something to eat.

The disciples were very surprised about this. All they could find was one tiny packed lunch, with five loaves of bread and two fish, which a little boy offered. That wouldn't be enough food for 5000 people, but they knew that Jesus could do amazing things (which we call 'miracles') and they trusted him to do what he said. So Jesus told the disciples to get the people to sit down in small groups. Then he gave each of the disciples a basket to hold. Jesus said a prayer and he sent the disciples out to all of the people.

Prompt your volunteers to take the baskets out, to share the imaginary food.

Would you believe it, the food just kept on coming! There was so much food that the people had more than enough to eat. In fact, when they had finished, there were twelve baskets of food left over. Jesus made sure that everyone had plenty.

Prayer

Thank you, God, that you always give us the things that we need, just as Jesus gave the crowds of people enough to eat in today's story. Amen

Songs

Songs today could include:

- 5000+ hungry folk (Ian Smale)

Take home

Suggest to your families that they may like to say grace—a prayer of thanks to God for the food that you have—when they share a meal together. You could suggest some simple prayers for your families to use if they would find this helpful.

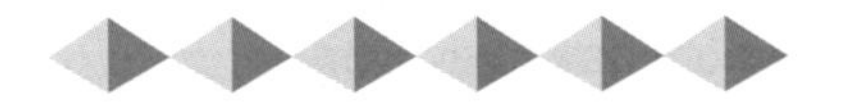

The good Samaritan

For the team

Refer to pages 6–8 to see how the activity areas work together

Session theme

This session explores another of Jesus' parables, with a lesson about how we should show love and care to everyone we meet, enabling the children to explore a key value that is relevant to all ages.

Bible text: Luke 10:25–37

Team prayer

Lord Jesus, today's story carries a real challenge to care for all people. Help us to model this care in our actions as well as in our teaching.

Activity areas

Sensory, tactile, malleable

Provide a selection of different coins, paper and wax crayons for the children to use to create rubbings of the coins. Encourage them to feel the coins first, by carefully rubbing their fingers over them.

Talk about the good Samaritan, who paid some of his own money to make sure that the man who had been hurt was looked after until he was well again.

Small world play

Provide a roadmap floor mat and a selection of toy vehicles for children to use to re-enact going on a long journey. As well as cars and buses, you could also provide some horses or donkeys to represent the way that the man in the story would have travelled.

Talk about children's own experiences of going on a long journey. Where did they go, how did they travel and who did they travel with? Explain that the man in the story today was badly hurt while he was on his journey.

Role play / dressing up

Set up a hospital or doctor's surgery where children can take turns to play a patient, doctor or nurse. You could include blankets on the floor to represent beds, toy medical cases, dressing-up outfits and an assortment of bandages for children to use to tend 'wounds'.

Talk about children's own experiences of being looked after when they have hurt themselves, perhaps at the hospital or by their parents. How good does it feel when someone takes care of us and makes things better?

Creative

For this activity, you will need a small craft box. Invite each child to paint their box green before sticking a white foam or card cross on to the lid. Give them a few plasters and an antibacterial wipe, to create their own small first aid kit.

Talk about the way that the good Samaritan took care of the man who had been injured. We can keep our first aid kits at home to be used when someone in our family gets hurt, too.

Books

Gather a selection of children's stories that talk about helping others, as well as children's Bibles and story books that retell the story of the good Samaritan. Other book themes could include journeys or hospitals.

Share the books with the children, reading the stories and talking about the things they discover in the books that they choose to look at.

Water

Add a small amount of washing-up liquid or hand soap to the water tray and provide some dolls' clothes for the children to 'wash' in the water tray. You could set up a washing line so that children can peg the washing out to dry.

Talk about the man in the story who was badly hurt and was left in a terrible mess. The good Samaritan treated him very kindly, taking him to a place where he could be cleaned up and looked after, so that he could get better.

Sand

Work with the children to dig into the sand and create a scene appropriate for the telling of today's story, with roadways, hills and valleys. You could provide some pebbles to represent rocks for the robbers to hide behind, and perhaps some figurines that could be used by the children to retell the story.

Talk about the route that the man was walking along: it was very dangerous, with robbers hiding, ready to jump out and attack him.

Puzzles, toys, games

In the selection of toys and games offered today, you could include things that focus on people who help us, such as doctors, nurses, police, fire fighters and so on.

Snack time

Story time

For this retelling, you will need a number of people figurines to represent the man on his journey, the robbers, the priest, the Levite, the good Samaritan and the innkeeper. Lay out a strip of brown fabric or paper to represent the road and invite the children and their carers to sit on the floor with you.

This is a story that Jesus told, to teach people how they should care for others. It's the story of a man who went on a journey.

Spread the roadway out in front of the children and hold up the man, walking him steadily along the road as you continue.

Suddenly, some robbers jumped out *(use these figures to push the man to the ground)*. They stole the man's money and hurt him badly. The poor man was left lying next to the road.

After a while, a priest came along *(move this figure along the road)*. You would expect a man who followed God to take care of the injured man, but he didn't—he just walked past.

Then another man who worked in the temple also came along *(move the next figure along the road, past the man)*. He saw the injured man lying beside the road but, instead of helping him, he walked past too.

Then another man walked along the road *(use the Samaritan figure to follow the road)*. This man was from a different town, and the people from the two towns were not good friends. Everyone would have expected this man to walk straight by, but he didn't. The man from Samaria stopped to help. He put bandages on the injured man's bumps and bruises and carefully helped him to get to a nearby hotel *(move both figures along the road to the innkeeper)*. When they got there, the Samaritan gave the innkeeper some money and asked him to help the man to get better again.

Jesus told this story to remind us that when we see somebody who needs our help, we should be ready to help them straight away and not walk past. Perhaps that means sharing our toys with someone we don't normally play with, or helping our parents with some jobs at home. We can all be good and kind, just like the Samaritan man in the story.

Prayer

Dear God, please help us to be good and kind, like the man in the story, and to look after people when they need our care. Amen

Songs

Songs today could include:

- Don't hide your light (Leanne Mitchell)

Take home

Encourage your families to take home the first aid kits that they have created, to keep in a safe place. The next time somebody needs a plaster, take out the box and use it as a reminder of today's story.

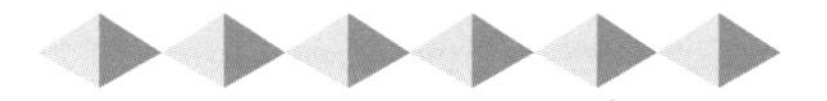

29 The lost sheep

For the team

Refer to pages 6–8 to see how the activity areas work together

Session theme

This is the first of three sessions exploring the 'lost and found' stories that remind us of our value in God's eyes.

Bible text: Luke 15:4–7

Team prayer

Lord Jesus, thank you that you know us all by name. Help us to celebrate with you when your lost sheep find their home.

Activity areas

Sensory, tactile, malleable

Source some sheep's wool in a variety of forms, including samples of wool recovered from a field, a fleece rug and a ball of spun wool. Encourage the children to use their hands to explore the differing textures. Combs could also be provided for children to tease through the wool.

Talk about the process followed to create a ball of wool and the things that we are able to make from sheep's wool.

Small world play

Create a farmyard scene with farm workers and a selection of toy animals, including sheep, along with animal pens, tractors and other appropriate figures, with which children can take care of the animals at the farm.

Talk about the different jobs that farmers do to take care of their animals—providing food, shelter and bedding. How do farmers keep their animals safe?

Role play / dressing up

Use a playpen to create a sheep pen, and provide a selection of stuffed toy sheep and shepherd outfits (perhaps from the nativity costume supply). Encourage children to round up the sheep into the pen, using a stuffed toy sheepdog. They could also count the sheep and give them food and water.

Talk about why the shepherd rounds up his sheep into the pen—to keep them safe.

Creative

Prepare card strips to be wrapped around the children's heads, some cotton wool balls, glue, and black sugar paper ears. Help children to cover the card strip with the cotton wool balls before attaching the ears. Staple the band together to fit around the child's head.

Talk about children's own experiences of sheep—their appearance, the sound they make, and the way they behave.

Construction

Provide a selection of clothes pegs, plastic straws, paper art straws and pipe cleaners. Invite children and carers to construct a model pen where the sheep could be kept safe.

Talk about how farmers bring their sheep together to keep them safe in a sheep pen, so that they cannot wander away and find themselves in danger.

Books

The book selection for this session should include children's Bibles and age-appropriate retellings of the story, along with information books about sheep. You could also include magazines or journals about sheep and farming, with photographs of different breeds of sheep that the children can discuss.

Share the books and magazines with the children, offering to read the stories and talking about the things they notice in the pictures.

Sand

Bury plastic toy sheep or laminated pictures of sheep in the sand for children to uncover, using their hands or the sand tools. Encourage children to count the sheep as they uncover them and to hide them once again for other children to find.

Talk about how excited the children feel when they find each of the sheep. Explain that the farmer was very excited, in the story, when he found his lost sheep.

Puzzles, toys, games

Provide a selection of farm animal-themed toys, puzzles and games, with a particular focus on sheep and shepherds.

Snack time

Story time

As you gather the children together for the story time, invite them to bring a sheep with them from the different activity areas and to sit with it on their lap while you tell the story. Alternatively, you could invite families, in advance of the session, to bring a toy sheep with them.

Let's take a look at all the sheep you have brought here. Look, there's a very woolly sheep, and look, there's a very big sheep. I wonder who has the smallest sheep, and who has a sheep with a curly fleece? Who can make a noise like a sheep?

This is a story that Jesus told about a shepherd who took care of all his sheep. How many sheep do you think we've got here now? Let's count them together: 1, 2, 3…

The shepherd in today's story had 100 sheep. Every day he looked after them, taking them to places where they could find food and water and keeping them away from danger. Every night he would count his sheep to make sure that they were all safe—1, 2, 3, 4, all the way up to 100. They were all safe and sound.

One night, when he counted his sheep, the shepherd found there was a problem. One of his sheep was missing. The shepherd loved all his sheep and wanted to keep them safe, so he set out to find the lost one. He searched in the bushes and he searched behind the rocks; he searched up the hillside and he searched in the valleys. He searched and searched a long, long way, for a long, long time—and eventually, when he thought there was nowhere else to look, he found his missing sheep.

Encourage children to cheer.

The shepherd was so happy to have found his sheep that he had a great big party. He invited all his friends and family to come and celebrate with him, because the sheep he loved so much was now safe again, back home where it belonged.

When Jesus told the story, he said that God loves us, just as the shepherd loves his sheep—and when a person comes back to God and does the right thing, the angels in heaven have a party to celebrate.

Prayer

Father God, thank you that you love us, just as the shepherd loves his sheep. Just as the shepherd takes care of his sheep, you take care of us too. Amen

Songs

Songs today could include the following adaptation of 'Baa, baa, black sheep':

Baa, baa, lost sheep,
Where have you gone?
Up hill, down hill,
And all round the town.
I'll search all day, and I'll search all night.
I'll keep on looking till I know you're all right.

Take home

Suggest that your families might like to visit a farm to see some sheep. Alternatively, they could play a game of Hide and Seek and talk about how it feels to be found.

30

The lost coin

For the team

Refer to pages 6–8 to see how the activity areas work together

Session theme

This is the second of three sessions exploring the 'lost and found' stories, which remind us all how much we are loved by God.

Bible text: Luke 15:8–10

Team prayer

Lord Jesus, thank you that each of us is loved and known by you. Help us to share this truth with the people we meet today.

Activity areas

Sensory, tactile, malleable

Provide play dough, rolling pins and a selection of coins for children to press into the dough, to make imprints. You could include foreign currency or play money, but do provide real British currency too, as it will be familiar to the children.

Talk about what you notice when you look closely at the coins and the imprints the children have created. Do they know the value of any of the coins? Which ones do they think are the most precious, and why?

Role play / dressing up

Set up a 'home corner', complete with a selection of items including brushes and brooms, dusters and toy vacuum cleaners. Encourage children and carers to tidy up and clean the area, putting everything back in its place.

Talk about how the children help to tidy up at home and why it is important to keep everything safe and in the right place. Ask the children if they have ever lost anything. How did they feel?

Creative

Provide some cupcakes, along with icing and a selection of sprinkles and other cake decorations, for children to use to decorate their own celebration cupcake.

Talk about the different reasons why we have parties and tell the children that there is a party in the story today. What is their favourite part of a party? What parties have they recently enjoyed?

Construction

Provide a large number of coins (toy currency, perhaps) and invite children and carers to have a go at building a tower of coins as high as they can, counting the coins as they place them on the tower until it topples over.

Talk about how precious the coins are and how we have to take care of them and make sure we do not lose them.

Books

Ensure that you have books about this story available for children to look at, along with age-appropriate children's Bibles.

Offer to read the story to any children who are interested, or talk about the pictures that they are looking at.

Sand

Hide some coins in the sand and provide sand tools for the children to use to hunt for the money. Encourage them to search carefully and to count the coins as they find them. Ask them to hide the coins again so that other children can have a go at finding them.

Talk about how the children feel when they find each coin. Why do they want to find them so much?

Puzzles, toys, games

The toys you provide today could include counting games and puzzles that encourage children to count to ten. You may also include money-related toys, such as tills and purses with toy money, or piggy banks.

Snack time

Story time

Today's story is told dramatically and involves the children in playing the different roles. You will need a small number of props, as detailed in the script. Make sure everyone is seated comfortably before you begin.

This is a story that Jesus told to help people understand how much God loves them. We can use this story to remember that message too. Everyone will have a part to play today. I need somebody to be the lady in my story *(choose a child, a mum or a female helper)*, and everyone else will be involved at the end.

Give everyone a party popper or blower, with the strict instruction not to use it until they are told to at the end of the story.

Once there was a lady who worked very hard and saved very hard. She had saved up ten coins.

Pass the ten coins to the lady and encourage everyone to count aloud as you do so.

One, two, three, four, five, six, seven, eight, nine, ten.

She kept the coins safe in her house.

Ask your lady to go and put the coins in a safe place.

Every day, she took her coins out and counted them.

Ask your volunteer to go back and collect the coins. Count them aloud together.

One, two, three, four, five, six, seven, eight, nine, ten.

As you give the coins back, to be returned to the safe place, secretly keep hold of one.

One day, the lady took her coins out to count them again.

Your volunteer will need to collect them again.

One, two, three, four, five, six, seven, eight, nine… that was all!

The tenth coin wasn't there. The lady was very worried. She searched high and low until she found it.

Give a dustpan and brush to your volunteer so that she can pretend to clean the stage area and search for the tenth coin. Find a way of revealing the hidden coin.

Wow! She has found it! After searching very hard, the lady found her lost coin. She counted them all carefully again…

One, two, three, four, five, six, seven, eight, nine, ten.

She was so happy to have all her coins back together safely again that she invited all her friends round for a party, to celebrate the news that the coin she had lost was now back safely where it belonged.

Invite everybody to pop their party poppers or blow their party blowers and cheer, clap and celebrate.

When Jesus told this story, he said, 'Just like this woman celebrated when her lost coin was found, the angels in heaven have a party every time someone comes back to God and does the right thing.'

Prayer

Thank you, God, that you love us even more than the lady in the story loved her coin. Help us always to stay close to you and to do the right thing. Amen

Songs

Songs and rhymes today could include:

- Ten silver coins (Ian Smale)
- The following variation on 'Ten green bottles':

Ten silver coins sitting on a shelf,
Ten silver coins sitting on a shelf,
And if one silver coin should accidentally fall,
There'd be nine silver coins sitting on a shelf.

Continue counting down with each verse.

Take home

Suggest that your families may like to count some coins together or make their own coin rubbings, as they remember the story.

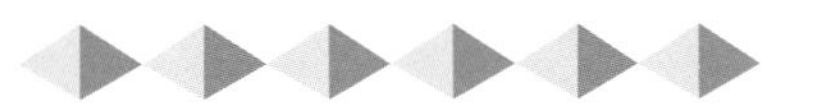

31

The prodigal son

For the team

Refer to pages 6–8 to see how the activity areas work together

Session theme

In this final session in the trilogy of 'lost and found' stories, we see a glimpse of the extremes of emotion experienced by the characters in the story, from sorrow and pain to joy and acceptance. We are reminded that we too can have a place in the story.

Bible text: Luke 15:11–32

Team prayer

Father God, thank you for loving us all the same, whether we stay by your side or travel far from home. May we celebrate with you when your children come back home.

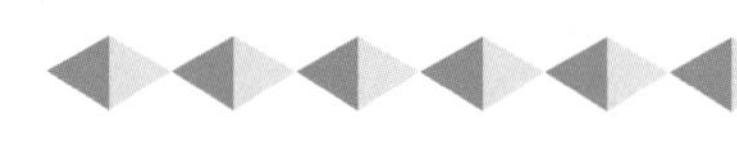

Activity areas

Sensory, tactile, malleable

Create some mud by mixing water with soil or with ground coffee, if preferred. Provide some small plastic pig figurines for children to play with in the mud.

Talk about how messy pigs can be and how they enjoy rolling in the mud. The son who left his father had to take care of pigs when all his money had gone. He would have got very messy too.

Small world play

Provide a farmyard scene, ensuring that the animals include toy pigs.

Talk about the different jobs that farmers do to take care of their animals. Which jobs would children like to try completing? Which jobs are less appealing? The son in the story had to do the worst job there was—looking after the pigs.

Role play / dressing up

Set up a party scene, with a table, paper plates and cups, and pretend food. Hang banners and balloons around the area and provide party hats for the children to wear.

Talk about children's own experiences of going to a party. The father in the story held a big party when his son came back home.

Creative

Before the session, colour some dry hollow pasta, such as penne or macaroni, using a variety of food colourings. Provide lengths of cord, wool or string and invite the children and carers to thread their own pasta necklaces or bracelets.

Talk about how the father in the story put a precious ring on his son's finger when he came home, to welcome him back into the family.

Construction

Provide a selection of props that the children can use to create a maze, such as tables and chairs or boxes and pallets. Make sure you have some appropriate objects that relate to the story, such as a bag of coins, a toy pig, a ring and so on, for the children to place within the maze.

Talk about each of the props as the children discover them, and discuss how they relate to the story.

Books

Display a variety of children's Bibles and books telling the story of the prodigal son, alongside books about families and pigs.

Share the books with children, as they wish, reading the stories requested and talking about things that the children find of interest.

Water

Add a small amount of hand soap or washing-up liquid to the water tray and provide a selection of plastic people figurines, perhaps with removable clothes. Invite the children to give the people a bath and wash their clothes before putting them to dry on a washing line or clothes dryer.

Talk about how messy the son in the story would have been when he got home, after looking after the pigs. His dad gave him a great big hug—and probably let him have a relaxing bath, too.

Puzzles, toys, games

Toys and games offered today could have a family theme, such as the card game where you need to collect each of the family members, as well as resources with a pig theme.

Snack time

Story time

Today's story is told dramatically and will need some volunteers to help. Three of your helpers will play the parts of the father and his two sons, primed to mime appropriately in response to the script as you narrate. You will also need a small group of children to be the partygoers and another small group of children to be the pigs. Provide a bag of coins, a cloak, a ring and some party blowers or party poppers, to be used at the appropriate points.

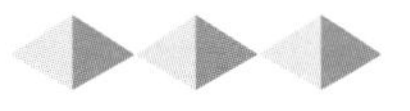

This is another story that Jesus told: There once was a man with two sons, who he loved very much. One day, the youngest son said to his dad, 'I know that one day I will be given half of all your money, but I don't want to wait. I want it now! Give me my share of the money so that I can go off and explore the world.' He was very rude, wasn't he?

The dad felt very sad when his son spoke to him like that, but he decided to give him the money and let him go and explore the world. So off the son went, off to the big city, where he made lots of new friends *(invite the partygoers to surround the son)*. He spent his money on expensive things and parties *(the volunteer could throw the coins up into the air)*. He always paid for his friends, so they liked him very much. But after a while, the money ran out—and when the money ran out, his new friends weren't interested in him any more, so they all went away.

The son had to get a job, but the only job he could find was to look after the pigs *(direct your volunteer towards the children playing the part of the pigs)*. He was now so poor and so hungry that he wanted to eat the pig food. This made the son stop and think. He knew that if he went back home and said 'sorry', his dad could give him a better life than this.

So the son set off back home. When he got there, he started to tell his dad that he was sorry. His dad gave him a big hug and told him how much he loved him. Then they had a party to celebrate!

Blow the party blowers and pop the party poppers.

The oldest son found it hard to understand why his dad wasn't angry with his brother. But his dad explained, 'I love you both very much, and now you are both back home with me. That makes me feel very happy.' God is like the dad in that story, who celebrates when one of his children come back to him.

Prayer

Thank you, God, that you love us, just like the dad did in today's story. Thank you that you welcome us into your family. Amen

Songs

Songs today could include:

- Father God, I wonder (Ishmael)

Take home

Suggest that your families may like to create a family painting or canvas this week, enjoying spending time together as a family.

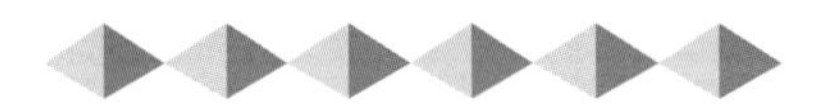

32

Jesus notices Zacchaeus

For the team

Refer to pages 6–8 to see how the activity areas work together

Session theme

This session explores what happened when Zacchaeus had a life-changing encounter with Jesus, reminding us that Jesus notices each of us and knows us all by name.

Bible text: Luke 19:1–10

Team prayer

Lord Jesus, when we encounter you, everything changes. Through this group, may we enable those who attend to discover that they are known and loved by you.

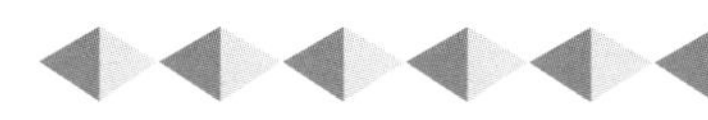

Activity areas

Sensory, tactile, malleable

Gather some pieces of bark or small logs and provide wax crayons and paper for children to use to create rubbings of the bark. Encourage children to explore how the bark feels when they run their fingers over it, as well as when they create an impression with the crayons.

Talk about Zacchaeus climbing up the tree to get a better view of Jesus, and how the bark would have felt against his hands and feet.

Small world play

Lay out a green piece of fabric and provide a large number of people figurines, along with a few trees, for children to use to re-enact today's story.

Talk about the huge crowd of people who wanted to see Jesus, and help the children to represent them with the play figurines.

Role play / dressing up

Set up a home area, where children can sit down together around a table to re-enact sharing a meal, using plastic plates, cups, cutlery and play food.

Talk about the children's own experiences of being invited to a special meal. Explain that people did not like Zacchaeus because he had done some bad things, but Jesus wanted to show Zacchaeus that he loved him, so he went to his house for tea.

Creative

Provide a number of plant pots, along with compost and some sunflower seeds for the children to plant. Encourage them to take care of the seeds and watch them grow when they go home.

Talk about how tall the sunflowers will grow, and about Zacchaeus, who was so short that he had to climb a tall tree to see Jesus.

Construction

Invite the children to work with you to create a large tree. If possible, use an alternative method to the one used in Session 2, perhaps using a large, strong cardboard tube, with sticks or thinner tubes as branches, or a flat tree drawn and cut from a large sheet of cardboard. Invite children to stick their bark rubbings on to the tree and to create paper leaves and add them to the branches. Stand the model tree securely in front of a chair to be used in the story retelling.

Talk about how Zacchaeus climbed a tree to see Jesus, because he was short and could not see over the crowds. Ask the children about their own experiences of being a short person in a busy, crowded place.

Books

Provide a selection of children's Bibles and retellings of the story. You could also provide some children's books in which the central character changes in the course of the story, perhaps from being mean or grumpy to being kind and generous, like Zacchaeus did.

Share the books with the children, offering to read the stories to them as they wish. Talk about the themes raised in the story books and the way that they relate to the story of Zacchaeus.

Sand

Bury a number of coins, play or real, for the children to uncover by sieving the sand. You could also provide small bags for the children to put the coins into.

Talk about Zacchaeus and how he had kept a lot of money that wasn't really his. When he met Jesus, he changed his ways and gave the money back.

Puzzles, toys, games

Provide a selection of games that involve children having to share fairly, perhaps sharing out cards or counters.

Snack time

Story time

Take the tree that you created in the construction area and attach it to a chair for somebody to stand on as they play the part of Zacchaeus. Invite the children and carers to come and sit in front of the tree. You will need a volunteer to play the part of Jesus, another to be Zacchaeus, and a group of children to play the part of the crowd.

I wonder if you've ever been somewhere that was very crowded or busy. Perhaps there were crowds of people waiting to see someone special? When Jesus was on earth, there were often crowds of people wanting to see him.

One day, Jesus was walking through the streets of Jericho when crowds of people came to see him. *Prompt the children to come close to Jesus.*

In Jericho, there lived a man called Zacchaeus. He was a little man, a man who nobody liked. It was his job to take people's money to give to the Romans, but instead of taking just the right amount, he would always take too much money and keep some of it for himself.

Zacchaeus wanted to see Jesus too, but, because he was so short, he couldn't see over the crowds of people. So Zacchaeus climbed up into a tree to see Jesus when he walked by.

And that is just what Jesus did—he walked along the street, right in front of the tree where Zacchaeus was sitting. When Jesus got to the tree, he stopped, looked straight up into the branches and said, 'Come down, Zacchaeus. I'm coming to your house for tea!'

Zacchaeus was very surprised when he heard Jesus' words. All the crowds were surprised, too. Everybody knew that Zacchaeus stole people's money, so why would Jesus want to spend time with a bad man like that?

But that's just what Jesus did. He went to Zacchaeus' house to have tea with him. Zacchaeus felt very special to be chosen by Jesus. He realised that the things he was doing weren't right, and he said, 'Jesus, thank you for spending time with me. I know now that I've done some really bad things, and I want to put things right. Today, I'm going to give people back the money I stole, and I'm going to give some money to the poor people too.'

And that's exactly what Zacchaeus did. Spending time with Jesus helped him to see how he could show Jesus' love to other people, just as Jesus had shown him love.

Prayer

Dear Jesus, thank you that you love us all, whether we are short like Zacchaeus or as tall as the trees. Thank you that you love us when we are good and when we do bad things, too. Please help us to be more like you every day. Amen

Songs

Songs today could include:

- Zacchaeus was a very little man (Anon)

Take home

Encourage your families to talk about the things they could do to show God's love to others.

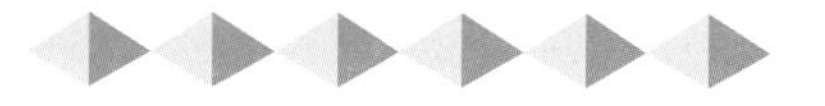

33

Palm Sunday

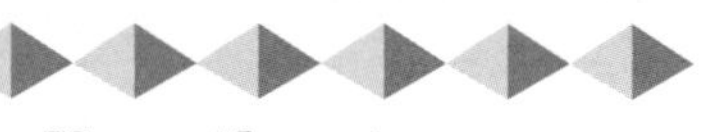

For the team

Refer to pages 6–8 to see how the activity areas work together

Session theme

The first session in the Easter narrative reminds us of Jesus the king, in his unlikely parade into Jerusalem. This session invites the children to share in celebrating the arrival of King Jesus.

Bible text: Matthew 21:1–11; Luke 19:40

Team prayer

Hosanna, King Jesus, welcomed in Jerusalem and welcomed here today.

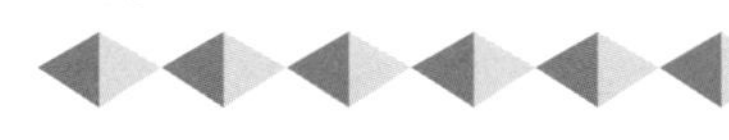

Activity areas

Sensory, tactile, malleable

Gather a selection of different leaves in a variety of shapes and sizes, and provide some paper and wax crayons. Invite the children and carers to create leaf rubbings on the paper.

Talk about the different shapes and sizes of leaf. Explain that, in today's story, the crowds of people found enormous leaves that they could wave, as if they were flags, to welcome Jesus.

Small world play

Create a road scene where children can re-enact the procession from the story or a procession with a king or queen, perhaps with a toy horse and carriage or limousine, as well as a donkey. Provide people figurines to line the streets and cheer their visitor.

Talk about the way you might expect a king or queen to travel. The crowds in today's story recognised Jesus as their king, even though he was only riding on a donkey.

Role play / dressing up

Provide a selection of royal costumes, including crowns, gowns and princess dresses, for children to dress up in.

Talk about how the royal family would wear special clothes like these for a special parade, but Jesus wore his ordinary clothes and rode on the back of a donkey. Why do you think he did that? Why do you think the people called him a king?

Creative

Provide a selection of pebbles, paint and paintbrushes, and invite the children to paint patterns, pictures and even words of praise, as they are able.

Talk about how Jesus told the rulers that if the crowds did not praise him, the stones would do so, because of his greatness.

Construction

Provide a selection of cushions, wooden planks, pallets, paving slabs and carpet tiles, with which the children can construct a pathway. Invite them to walk along it carefully.

Talk about Jesus' journey into Jerusalem and how we remember this special story.

Books

Gather a selection of books about kings and queens, as well as children's Bibles and books that retell today's story.

Share the books with the children, reading the stories as they wish and comparing the kings and queens in the books with King Jesus.

Water

Provide different leaves that the children can use to explore in the water, by scooping, dragging and splashing.

Talk about the people in today's story and how they would have used large leaves to wave, because they didn't have flags or banners.

Puzzles, toys, games

The toys and games offered today could relate to the theme of royalty or journeys, including a variety of different vehicles.

Snack time

Story time

Involve all your children and carers in the retelling of today's story, by asking them to sit in two rows, facing one another and leaving a wide gap down the middle. Encourage them to hold their jackets, cardigans or coats, ready to lay them on the floor, and to wave the leaf rubbings that were made in the 'Sensory, tactile, malleable' area, as Jesus moves between the rows. You will need a volunteer to play the part of Jesus and a hobby horse donkey for him to ride on.

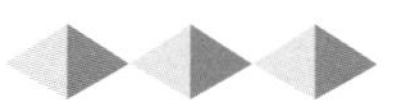

Whenever Jesus visited a town, crowds of people would come to see him. Do you remember the story we heard last week, when Zacchaeus had to climb up a tree to see Jesus? This is another story about the crowds of people who came to see him.

One day, Jesus and his disciples were visiting the city of Jerusalem. Jesus told his disciples where they could find a donkey for him to borrow, to ride into the city. As Jesus got close to the city, the crowds gathered, ready to see him.

Jesus should ride the donkey down through the middle of the crowds, slowly, allowing time for the children to join in with the cheering, as prompted (see the script below).

'Here comes our king!' they called, because they knew that Jesus had been sent by God to be a very special king. 'Hooray for King Jesus!' they shouted. Some people took their coats off and put them on the ground for the donkey to walk over. Others waved palm branches in the air. 'Hosanna, Hosanna!' they all shouted, as King Jesus arrived in the city of Jerusalem.

Jesus was no ordinary king. He did not ride in a chariot. He wasn't wearing a crown. He didn't bring an army to take over the city. He just rode a donkey, while all the people cheered.

Prayer

King Jesus, thank you that you came to earth to be our special king. When we shout 'Hooray' and 'Hosanna', help us to remember just how special you are. Amen

Songs

Songs today could include:

- Shake my shaker (Nigel Hemming)
- What noise shall we make? (Lucy East)

Take home

You could suggest that your families may like to read the stories from the Holy Week narrative this week, perhaps providing story books and Bibles for the children to take home with them.

34

A very sad day and a very happy day

For the team

Refer to pages 6–8 to see how the activity areas work together

Session theme

This session explores what is undoubtedly the central episode to God's big story, bringing God's new hope to the people he loves so much.

Bible text: Matthew 26—28

Team prayer

Lord Jesus, today we remember your death and celebrate your resurrection. Help us to share the great hope that this story offers to all people.

Activity areas

Sensory, tactile, malleable

Before the session, make copies of the blank face template on to card (see page 124) and laminate them. Prepare some play dough in a range of colours, appropriate for adding facial features, and invite the children to add hair, eyes and mouths to the face shapes, thinking about different emotions.

Talk about the different stages of the story and the different feelings that people would have experienced at each point. For older children, try to expand the vocabulary beyond 'happy' and 'sad'.

Small world play

Begin to create a basic Easter garden, which children can use to retell the different stages of the story. Children could tie sticks together to form crosses that they can push into the soil base, perhaps on a hill or mound shape. They could dig out an empty tomb shape with a flat stone placed in front of it, to represent the large stone in the story.

Talk about each stage of the story as they put the scene together, helping them to recall the details of the narrative and to reflect on what each part of the story means to us.

Creative

Provide a number of card crosses and a selection of collage materials, glue and scissors, so that the children can decorate a cross to display at home. You could provide some examples of crosses, perhaps those used in your own church, as a stimulus for this activity.

Talk about why the cross is such an important image for Christians and why it is so special.

Construction

Invite the children to help you construct a model of the tomb. This could be done by building a frame from chicken wire and working with the children to cover it in papier mâché. Alternatively, you could make it from cardboard boxes or use a dome tent covered with a blanket. Remember to create a circular 'stone' to place at the entrance.

Talk about the fact that the tomb represents a sad part of the story, but there is also happiness, as Jesus overcame death when the tombstone was rolled away.

Books

Provide a selection of children's story Bibles and books that retell the Easter story at an age-appropriate level.

Read the stories to the children, as they wish, and discuss the things that interest them.

Water

Provide some red hearts in assorted sizes, made from thin foam, and some washable felt-tip pens. Invite the children and carers to scribble on the hearts before placing them in the water. Provide brushes, sponges or flannels, which can be used to 'clean' the hearts.

Talk about the two reasons why Jesus died at Easter—because he loves us so much and because, by dying for us, he gives us a fresh start, getting rid of all the bad things that we do. Cleaning the hearts in the water reminds us of this fresh start.

Sand

Source some small plastic eggs, as used in an egg hunt. Place a small chocolate egg into each one, as a treat, along with a symbol of the Easter story, such as a paper or wooden cross. Invite the children to use their hands or small spades to dig for the eggs.

Talk about the things that the eggs contain and how they relate to the Easter story. Tell the children that the chocolate eggs are a treat at Easter, but God's love for us is so much more precious.

Puzzles, toys, games

Your church may have a number of resources that are used to explore the Easter narrative, which could be brought out to support this session. Other toys could focus on themes of love and new life.

Snack time

Story time

For this story retelling, you will need four fabric circles (red, dark green, black and light green, large enough to act as background to the rest of the props, as explained below); a row of five concertina-folded people (with the central figure coloured to represent Jesus); a small wooden cross; an empty tomb shape, perhaps made from clay; a round stone; a small model table (dolls' house size) and a small model sword.

Invite the children and carers to sit in a large circle, so that you can place the props in the middle, visible to all. Begin the story by laying out the red circle to one side and placing the concertina people on top of it, with the model table.

While Jesus was on earth, he spent time with his special friends, teaching them about God and how to live life his way. One day, Jesus and his disciples were enjoying a special meal together when Jesus told his friends that he didn't have much time left with them on earth. Soon he would be leaving them. Jesus' friends felt confused.

Pause. Place the dark green circle next to the red one, and, as you tell the next part of the story, move the people across, putting the sword on the green circle at the appropriate moment.

When their meal was finished, Jesus and his disciples went out to a hillside so that Jesus could talk to God, his Father. While they were there, some soldiers came, with swords and weapons, and took Jesus away from his friends. Tear the concertina people to separate Jesus from the other figures.

Jesus' disciples felt very scared.

Pause. Place the black circle next to the dark green circle, and move the people across. At the appropriate moment, take the Jesus figure and lay it on top of the cross.

The soldiers and rulers did not believe the things that Jesus taught about God. Jesus was put on a cross to die. Jesus' disciples felt very sad.

Pause. Place the light green circle next to the black circle. Put the tomb on to this circle, with the stone across the front. Move the people and the props at the appropriate moments.

Jesus was put into a tomb with a heavy stone laid across the front, but three days later, when Jesus' friends came to visit his grave, they found that the stone had been rolled away and Jesus wasn't in the tomb any more. Jesus was not dead; he had come back to life. Jesus' friends were back together with their very special friend and they were very, very happy.

Prayer

Thank you, Jesus, that you died on the cross so that we can be your friends again. Thank you that you didn't stay dead, but came back to life. Amen

Songs

Songs today could include:

- Good news (Cindy Rethmeier)
- Lord, I lift your name on high (Rick Founds)

Take home

Consider inviting your families to join you for a special Easter celebration service or community event.

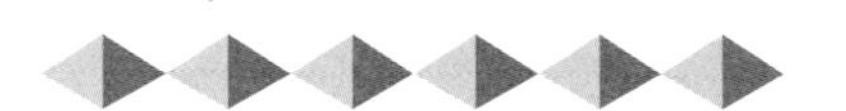

35

Jesus returns to heaven

For the team

Refer to pages 6–8 to see how the activity areas work together

Session theme

This session reminds us that Jesus' story did not reach its conclusion with the events of Easter. There came a time when Jesus' direct work on earth was complete and he could return home.

Bible text: Acts 1:6–11

Team prayer

Lord Jesus, today we remember how your disciples may have felt when the time came for you to return to heaven. Thank you for the gift of the Holy Spirit, which means that we never need to experience that anxiety.

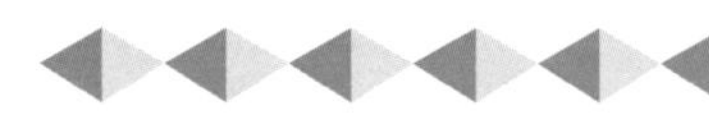

Activity areas

Sensory, tactile, malleable

Prepare some blue play mats (perhaps laminated pieces of blue card) and mix cornflour and water until you get an appropriately squishy consistency. Encourage children to squish and mould the gloop to create clouds on the play mats.

Talk about the different-shaped clouds that you see when you look at the sky.

Small world play

Set up a dolls' house and provide a selection of appropriate figurines for the children to play 'homes' with.

Talk about how you feel when you are at home. Why is home such a special place for your family?

Role play / dressing up

Set up a 'home corner', with familiar items that the children will have at home. The area could include a kitchen with cooking implements, dolls and cots for them to sleep in, and other household equipment.

Talk about the things the children do when they go home. How do they help to make any visitors feel welcome?

Creative

Provide catalogues, scissors, glue, paper and pencils. Invite children and carers to create a collage of 'home' by cutting out pictures of furniture and familiar items and sticking them on the paper. Be prepared to help with the cutting.

Talk about the things that make home special to the children. Which is your favourite room in your house? Why?

Construction

Provide building bricks and invite the children and carers to build their own model house. Encourage them to be imaginative, building as unusual a house as they can.

Talk about what sort of house they would build if they could. What rooms would they have in their dream home? How would they make their home special?

Books

Provide a selection of children's books about Jesus' life on earth, as well as children's Bibles.

Talk about the stories that children remember from the last few weeks. Which is their favourite story about Jesus? Offer to read any stories to the children.

Sand

Provide some small items for the children to hide in the sand. Invite them to take turns to hide something for the other children to find.

Talk about how it feels to be able to see the object, and how different the children feel when it has 'disappeared'. How do these feelings relate to today's story?

Water

Provide some bubble mixture, some small bubble wands and some larger hoops, which children can use to blow bubbles into the air. Watch how the bubbles float up into the sky before disappearing.

Talk about how the bubbles remind us that Jesus went up to heaven and disappeared.

Puzzles, toys, games

Today, you could set out some of the toys that have been popular over the last few weeks, to remind the children of the stories you have heard from Jesus' time on earth. You could also have some helium balloons with ribbons tied to them, so that children (under close supervision) can experience the way the balloons pull upwards when you try to hold them down.

Snack time

Story time

This story will work best if you have some small figurines to represent Jesus and his disciples. Sit everybody around in a circle and introduce the play figures before starting the story.

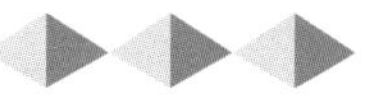

Today we are going to hear another story about Jesus and his disciples. You might remember some of the things Jesus did with his disciples.

If the children can remember any stories, encourage them to share them.

Do you remember about the very sad day when Jesus died? And the very happy day when Jesus came back to life? Today we are going to hear what happened next. This is the very last story about

Jesus and his time on earth.

One day, Jesus appeared to his disciples and asked them to go for a walk with him.

Move the figurines around at the appropriate moments in the story, using a piece of green fabric as a background.

He said to them, 'I've got one more important message to share with you. You need to go to all the places in the world, across the sea to different countries and places you have never even heard of before. Everywhere you go, tell the people you meet all about me. Tell them about the things I did when I was with you. Tell them about the people that I made better. Tell them the stories I have told you. Tell them how much I love them.'

The disciples listened carefully to what Jesus said. 'I need to go now, back home to heaven to be with my Father. Don't be afraid; I am going to send a special helper to be with you, to help you be brave and do the special job I have given you. You will never be alone.'

When he had finished talking, Jesus went up, up, up, past the top of the trees, past the clouds, way up into the sky and back to his home in heaven, to be with Father God. The disciples were very surprised and a little bit scared, but they knew that Jesus was going to send a special helper to be with them, so they went home and waited for the special helper to arrive.

Prayer

Dear God, thank you that you are always with us, everywhere we go. We do not need to be afraid. Amen

Songs

Songs today could include:

- Lord, I lift your name on high (Rick Founds)

Take home

Suggest that families spend some time talking about what makes their homes special and about times when they have had to say 'goodbye' to somebody special.

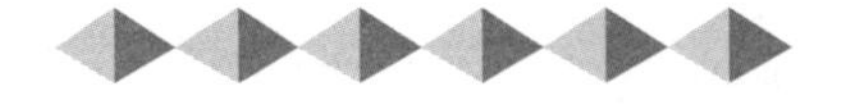

36

God sends his helper

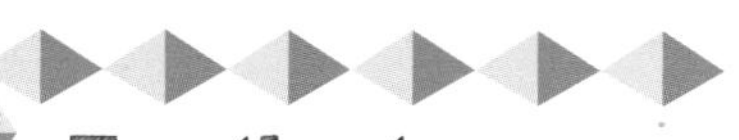

Refer to pages 6–8 to see how the activity areas work together

For the team

Session theme

This final session brings God's story to a conclusion with the events of Pentecost and the gift of the Holy Spirit, who gave the disciples authority to share God's story on that day and gives us the same authority today.

Bible text: Acts 2

Team prayer

Holy Spirit, we welcome you here among us. May we speak with power and authority as we share God's story with all those we meet.

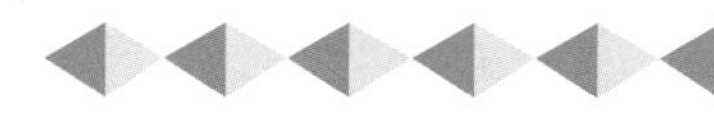

Activity areas

Sensory, tactile, malleable

In a shallow tray, mix some red, orange and yellow poster paints with water and washing-up liquid. Provide straws and invite the children to blow bubbles in the mixture before laying a piece of paper over the top to make a print. (Make sure they do not accidentally inhale the mixture.)

Talk about how the Holy Spirit blew as a wind into the room, rather like we have blown air into the bubbles. Talk about the colours of the paint and how they remind us of the flames.

Small world play

Lay out a world map as a base and provide a selection of small figures of people from around the world, perhaps with appropriate food items for the children to explore.

Talk about the different countries as they are represented and explain that, because of today's story, people from all over the world could hear the story of Jesus.

Role play / dressing up

Provide dressing-up clothes from around the world, such as Indian saris and African or Spanish outfits. Try to include costumes from the different countries represented by the children attending.

Talk about the different countries represented by the children in your group and the different languages that they can speak. Explain that, in today's story, God gave people the ability to speak in many different languages.

Creative

Copy the pinwheel template on to card (see page 126). Invite children and carers to decorate the shape with crayons or felt-tip pens and then attach it to a length of wooden dowel with a pin to make a pinwheel. (Alternatively, prepared kits can be purchased, which give children everything they need to make a pinwheel.) Demonstrate how they can blow the sails to help it go round.

Talk about the great wind that blew when the Holy Spirit arrived. The pinwheel helps us to see the effect of the wind, although we cannot see the wind itself.

Books

Books provided today should include children's Bibles, as well as books about Pentecost, the gifts of the Spirit and the fruit of the Spirit. You could also offer books about the weather, fire and different languages.

Read the books to the children, as they wish, and talk about the things that they find interesting.

Water

Provide a collection of boats with sails, which can be blown across the water. Simple sailboats can be made using plastic tubs, straws and paper sails, if you are unable to source any complete boats.

Talk about the way that the boats move when they are blown, just like large sailboats, which depend on the wind to move them.

Sand

Provide wet sand, buckets and spades and invite the children to build a sandcastle before inserting a small flag or pinwheel in the top. Encourage the children to blow the pinwheel or flag to make it move in the breeze.

Talk about how the wind blows flags and pinwheels when they are set up on the beach. When the Holy Spirit arrived, there was a loud noise like a rushing wind.

Puzzles, toys, games

Toys and games offered today could include some that relate to different countries and cultures, as well as jigsaw puzzle maps.

Snack time

Story time

For this storytelling, you will need twelve people shapes cut from light-coloured paper, some strips of brown paper to represent two walls and a roof surrounding the people, and twelve flame shapes cut from red or orange paper. Attach a small amount of sticky tack to the back of each flame.

Invite the children and carers to sit in a circle so that they can all see the props. Display the twelve people shapes, surrounded by the strips of brown paper to fence them in, as though they were inside a house.

After Jesus had gone back to heaven, his friends were hiding in a house. They were a bit nervous about what to do, now that Jesus had gone. Suddenly, a great big wind blew inside the house *(encourage the children to add suitable sound effects)*. The disciples were very scared.

After the wind, little flames came and sat on each of the disciples' heads *(attach the flames to the people shapes with the sticky tack)*. But this was no ordinary fire: it didn't burn the disciples. This was

God's Holy Spirit, coming to help the disciples to live life the way that God wanted them to, and to give them power so that they could talk bravely about Jesus to people who hadn't met him.

Now, the disciples felt very brave. They left the building *(remove the brown paper strips)* and went out into the streets *(spread the people shapes out in the space)*. God gave them special abilities to talk in all sorts of languages that they had never even heard before, so that the people in the crowds could all understand what they were saying.

Many, many people heard about Jesus for the first time, and lots and lots of people decided that they too wanted to start following God. So God's special message spread.

Pass the people shapes to the children and ask them to pass them around as you continue.

God's story started spreading that day, and it still spreads today. This is how we know about Jesus too. We can hear this story because God's Holy Spirit makes people brave enough to share the story, and we can share the story with our friends because God's Holy Spirit will make us brave too.

Prayer

Dear God, thank you for your story, and thank you for your Holy Spirit, who makes people brave enough to talk about you and changes people to be more like you. Amen

Songs

Songs today could include:

- Father, we adore you (Terry Coelho)

Take home

You may like to suggest that your families find new opportunities to talk to other people about Jesus, praying that the Holy Spirit will help them.

Templates

All templates can be downloaded at www.barnabasinchurches.org.uk/9780857463814

Playdough mat: face

Playdough mat: empty altars

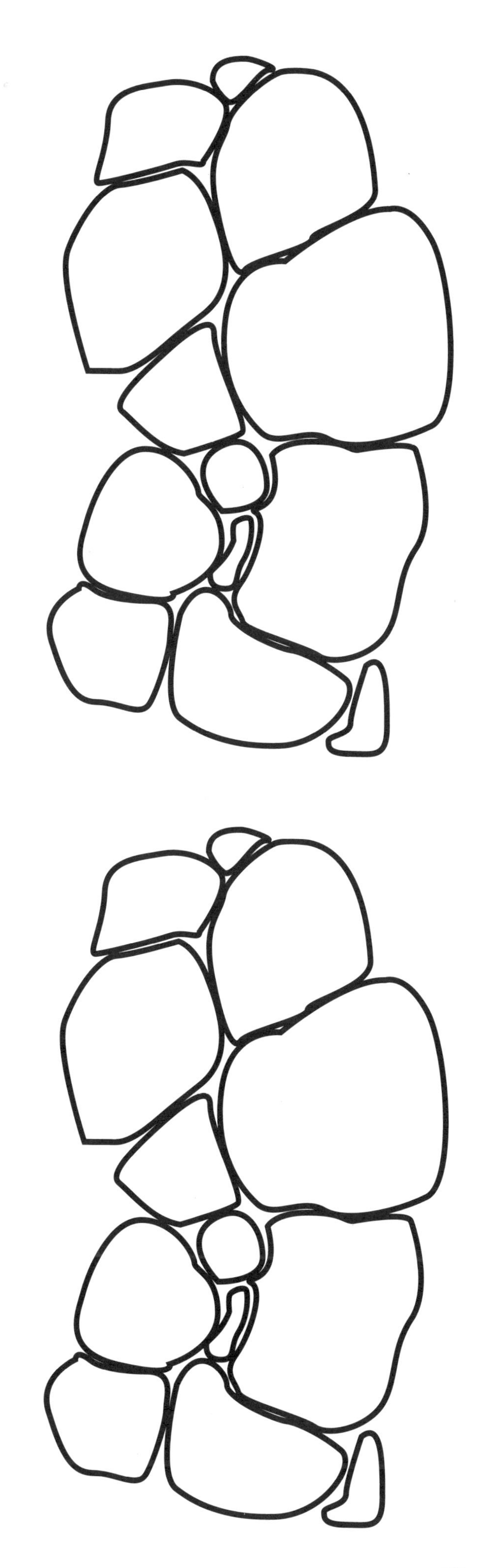

Dove

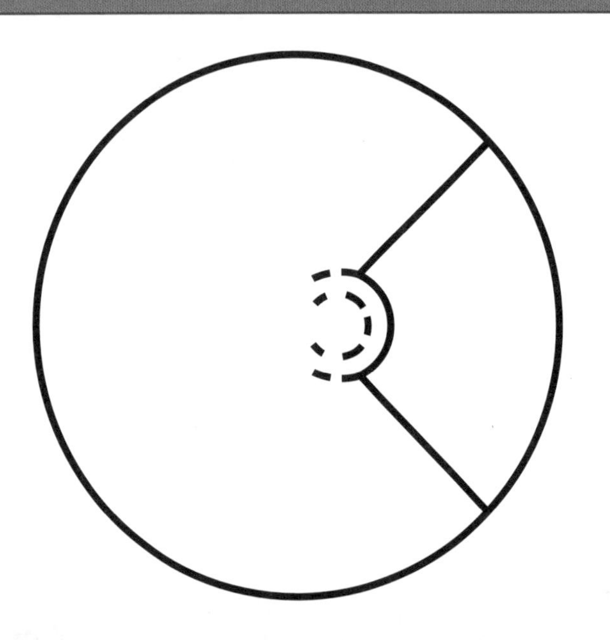

Angel

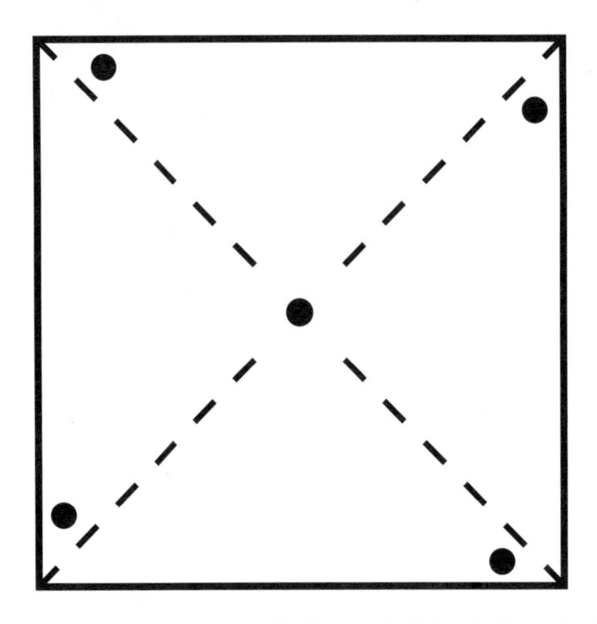

Pinwheel

Playdough mat: Jesus' baptism